Make It Memorable

Make It Memorable

Writing and Packaging TV News with Style

Bob Dotson

Bonus Books, Inc.
Chicago, Illinois

04   03   02   01   00   5   4   3   2   1

Library of Congress Control Number: 00-107291
ISBN: 1-56625-158-3

Bonus Books, Inc.
160 East Illinois Street
Chicago, Illinois 60611

Printed in the United States of America

To Linda and Amy,
who bookend my life
and prop me up

Contents

Foreword

The power of the written word is alive and well!

That's what I think when I watch one of Bob Dotson's stories. He is a craftsman who blends fascinating subjects with dramatic images and thought-provoking words. The result is a story that grabs and holds viewers' attention.

In this age of rapid-fire events and "get it on the air now" coverage, Bob's work stands out as artistic and mature. The perfect combination of information and intelligence.

Read this book. Learn from a master.

MATT LAUER
CO-HOST, THE *TODAY* SHOW

Acknowledgments

Writing is a solitary profession. Television is not. Many talented journalists work with me on my stories and help to shape them.

A special thanks to those whose efforts are highlighted on these pages—Dave Riggs, Laurie Singer, Amy Wasserstrom, John Hyjek, Rob Kane, James Townley, Cathy Romine, Darrell Barton, Bob Brandon, Bruce Bernstein, Craig White, Mike Sulzberger, Sylvia Oberlander, Ned Judge, Bill Wheatley, Cheryl Gould, Jeff Zucker, David Doss, Jonathon Wald.

I also want to thank Professor Fred Shook, my lifelong friend and mentor, whose advice still guides my work and echoes throughout these pages.

Finally, I thank NBC News for taking a chance on a kid with red hair and freckles and sticking with him until his hair turned gray.

BOB DOTSON

NEW YORK, NEW YORK

Make It Memorable

Introduction

BY MERVIN BLOCK

Want to be another Bob Dotson? Don't. Only Noah wanted two of a kind. As good as Bob is, the world is content with one Bob Dotson. But the broadcasting world does need more reporters with Bob's ability to tell stories. Not *tall* stories. Short stories. True stories. Good stories.

As a storyteller, Bob excels. He knows how to tell stories simply, clearly, skillfully. He tells them on NBC News. Often, they're not spot news. Or hot news. Or hard news. But he can make them news.

And Bob knows how to tell other pros *how* he he does it. So a good way for newbies, oldbies and wannabes to improve their skills is to see Bob Dotson, hear Bob Dotson and, now, *read* Bob Dotson.

When Bob spoke at the 1998 convention of the Radio-Television News Directors Association, he was such a hit that RTNDA scheduled him the next year for *two* sessions. The title: "I

Want to Write Like Bob Dotson." I was curious, so last year I made it a point to catch him in person.

The session I attended was in a large room with seats for 250 people. When I showed up, every seat was taken, the sitting-on-the-floor space was taken, and the standing room was taken. The place was so jammed I figured they were giving out door prizes. But my only luck was in being able to squeeze into the outermost edge of the standees—with no chance of becoming a sittee. Despite my discomfort in the crush, I was fortunate to have what Broadway theaters call an obstructed view. (Yes, I should have arrived on the dot, son.)

Bob made an arresting presentation. He played videotapes of his stories and told how and why he did what he did—in reporting, in interviewing, in writing, in editing, in packaging. He was so effective I wrote to my publisher, Aaron Cohodes, and suggested he ask Bob to write a book. So Aaron did, and Bob did. And this is it.

You can't get ready for prime time by going through one book, taking one course, attending one workshop, or even doing all those things. There's more to writing than that. But if you mean business, if you're all business, if you have the necessary equipment—and I don't mean a PC, a printer or a pager—you *can* become a far better story-teller.

In this book, Bob tells how—how he approaches a story, how he avoids the herd, how he thinks for himself. So if you want to find out how, here's a good place to learn some lessons. But don't try to *be* Bob Dotson. And don't try to be a copy. Be an original.

MERVIN BLOCK
WRITING COACH

Section One

My grandmother worries about my life's work. The first time she got a chance to see one of my stories on the *NBC Nightly News*, I called to ask her what she thought.

"Did you watch my story on Tom's show tonight?"

"Of course."

"Well, what did you think?"

There was a long pause at the other end of the line. Then she mumbled, "Bobby, I think you ought to learn a trade."

"A trade!"

"Yes, they're not going to keep paying you for two minutes of work a week!"

My grandmother is now a news director in Milwaukee. She wants twelve live shots from me after I finish this book.

But, seriously, I work in the real world just like you. We're all faced with constant deadlines these days. The twenty-four hour news clock slices time too thin for thought.

There always seems to be someone in New York who has had eight hours sleep and has something for me to do—*Nightly News*, *Today*, *Dateline*, CNBC, MSNBC, Internet. I've been in more motel rooms than the Gideon Bible. That's a lot of travel. It's not unusual for me to do fifty-nine stories in one month, average ninety hours a week.

Wherever I go these days, I hear a disturbing chorus of complaints from other journalists:

"Knowing is no longer a big priority in our newsroom. Appearing to know, you build your career."

"We parrot the same three facts on live shots throughout the day, because there's so little time to do much reporting."

Some say newsroom stress levels are at an all-time high.

"We're living our worst nightmare. The whole world is watching and we're unprepared."

No question, journalism is changing. Everything I first learned about this business is now in a museum. Typewriters. Film cameras. Hot splicers. Every tool, every technique is different.

Even the longer stories I love must now be done at the speed of spot news. Given our ever-shrinking deadlines, how can we produce these reports with a bit of style? What follows are a few tips to help us work faster and smarter. These are not my ideas. They are lessons I've learned from watching the most successful people in this business. A few tricks to save time, so you'll have more time to give your story some style.

"ONE THING IS CERTAIN..."

The news business is so complicated these days, it's a lot like a circus. Every night after the show, we all sit around and congratulate one another because we managed to get live shots from all over town. In other words, we got the circus tent up. But we sometimes overlook the fact that nobody tunes in to watch the tent. What they've come to see and hear are our stories. Unfortunately, the technical aspect of our business is now so complex, storytelling is sometimes the last thing we consider during our workday. It gets scant attention in most newsrooms. Here are three suggestions to make your stories better even under the tightest deadline.

The Rule of Threes and Filling the Silence

I've done thousands of interviews in the past three decades and have noticed a pattern to people's responses. They nearly always answer a question three times. First, they tell you the answer they want you to hear. Second, they explain their answer. Third, they blurt out a soundbite—if you wait a beat before jumping in with the follow-up question. Let the silence grow. Silence makes people uncomfortable. They suspect you still don't understand their answer. That's when they put their thoughts into sharp focus.

Uncomfortable silence helps you get a more memorable, shorter soundbite. And yet, what's the one thing we don't do in this age of live shots? We *never* stop talking. That's why we end up relying on professional speakers—lawyers and pundits—people who can give us the soundbites we expect, even if we interrupt them. The problem with that is, *everybody* gets the same soundbites. Often predictable. Sometimes boring.

The Non-Question/Question

How do you get unique soundbites? Try asking the Non-Question/Question. I learned this trick from a photojournalist named Scotty Berner, who used the technique one time to scoop the world press. A dozen crews were staking out the home of a young pilot in Lubbock, Texas. The boy's father was the leader of the Iranian government at the time, a dying king who had just been deposed. Every network wanted a soundbite from the son. Only Scotty got it, simply by asking the Non-Question/Question.

The young pilot was going to school in Lubbock. He lived off campus, his home heavily guarded. The boy was never seen. Stakeout crews sat day after day. Just before sunset one evening, Scotty saw a young man walking down the street who didn't look like he grew up in West Texas.

Scotty shouldered his camera. Quietly stepped away from the gaggle of photographers. Wandered down to talk to the boy. He noticed the fellow was looking at flowers.

Scotty spoke softly as he approached, so the other crews couldn't hear the conversation. "Aren't those beautiful lilies?"

The young man answered. "Yes, they really are."

Then, Scotty turned on the camera and said, "I used to work in a flower shop before I became a news photographer."

Now, the boy knew for sure what must have been obvious: Scotty was a news cameraman. But, so far, they were simply talking about flowers.

Watch what happens, though, as they continue to talk. Scotty subtly steers the conversation to the subject of fathers.

"My dad used to love flowers."

The young man said, "Yeah, my dad loves flowers, too."

Scotty looked at the lilies and added quietly, "My father died two years ago after a long illness," which was true.

That prompted the young man to say, "My dad is real sick, too."

Now here comes the trick—the Non-Question/Question. Scotty said softly, "I miss my dad."

"Me, too," the young man answered, lost in thought.

Scotty let the silence between them build. Finally, the man looked up at the camera and in the next ten seconds gave Scotty an exclusive, unique soundbite, even though no question had ever been asked.

"My father will be taken to Panama. He is a man without a country. It is so sad...."

Scotty *still* didn't know for sure if this boy was the king's son, until a couple of minutes later when a bodyguard at the young man's house bobbed up over a hedge, noticed the boy and began shouting.

"He's out! He's out!"

A half dozen guards ran down the driveway.

Scotty knew better than to start arguing First Amendment freedom with guys who are carrying their Second Amendment freedom. Instead, he simply turned his camera on them, shooting the pictures he'd need to set up the young man's soundbite.

Scotty had scooped the world press without ever asking a question.

Later, he explained how he did it:

"With the Non-Question/Question, you put people at ease. Talk about what is going on in their lives. Then, gradually bring the subject around to the topic you want to discuss."

Instead of jumping out of the truck with all your gear, breathlessly waving microphones at people, simply walk up and say, "Hi, I just want to introduce myself." If the scene is emotional, apologize for intruding. If the story subject is busy, talk about what he's doing. "Hey, I painted my house last year, too...."

Review

We all can tell better stories immediately by remembering:

- The Rule of Threes
- Filling the Silence
- The Non-Question/Question

Script #1: "Lives Lost"

On the next page is an example of what those three techniques can produce, a story about five little girls shot dead in a Jonesboro, Arkansas, schoolyard. See if you can spot the Non-Question/Question.

"LIVES LOST" / TODAY SHOWSIDE
JONESBORO, ARKANSAS
TOTAL RUNNING TIME 3:28
CORRESPONDENT: BOB DOTSON
PRODUCER: LAURIE SINGER

[KATIE COURIC]
Murder puts some places on the map, as unfair as that is. Everyone now knows where Jonesboro is. And what happened there. But something got lost in our reporting. We told you little about the girls who died. They became—simply—tragic symbols of what can go terribly wrong. They were more than that, of course.

Here's NBC's Bob Dotson.

=-=-=-=-=-=-=-=-=-script-=-=-=-=-=-=-=-=

CLASSMATES OF THE DEAD
STUDENTS SITTING IN AN OLD GYM,
BUILT IN THE 1920'S

KIDS THUMBING THRU YEARBOOKS
BOY ASKS A CLASSMATE:
"WHAT GRADE WAS SHE IN 1994?"

[Narration]
Sometimes the yearbook of life closes too soon.

SOT: "HERE'S BRITTHANY VARNER..."

BLK.WHT PHOTOS GIRLS	[Narration] We are left with grainy pictures and long-lens grief. VO/SOT: "IT'S JUST WEIRD THEY WERE THE ONES TO DIE." [Narration] No way to measure a loss. VO/SOT: "THEY WERE PROBABLY THE NICEST KIDS IN SCHOOL."
LAYERED SHOTS OF CRIME SCENE/GRAVE/FLOWERS	[Narration] The four little girls who died in that Jonesboro schoolyard were more than what happened to them. They were small-town kids with barefoot voices ... a lot like these.
GIRLS PHOTOS—MIXED WITH FRIENDS SOUND	(STEPHANIE) SOT: "SHE WAS A KIND-HEARTED PERSON AND SHE CARED ABOUT PEOPLE." (PAIGE) SOT: "SHE WAS A GOOD BASKETBALL PLAYER AND VOLLEYBALL PLAYER." (COLBY BROOKS) SOT: "YOU KNEW SHE WOULD HAVE KICKED EVERYONE'S BUTT." (BRITTHANY) SOT: "SHE WAS FRIENDLY. SHE HAD A GOOD SENSE OF HUMOR. SHE LOVED TO SMILE."

(NATALIE)
SOT: "SHE HAS PRETTY EYES."
SOT: "SHE WOULD ALWAYS CARRY
HER BIBLE TO SCHOOL."

WIDE SHOT OF DOTSON WALKING ON
BASKETBALL COURT

(BOB DOTSON / STANDUP)

BOB DOTSON
NBC NEWS
SUPER IN   1:06
       OUT 1:15

"Their friends thought you might like to
see where ...

CUT TO CLOSEUP OF DOTSON

Paige Herring perfected her jump shot.
And Natalie Brooks practiced her cheers.
Stephanie Johnson sang her first sweet
song right here.
And Britthany Varner gave her a hug.
She always had hugs for her friends."
{STANDUP ENDS}

(GIRL'S VOICE)
SOT:"IT'S REALLY SAD NOW THAT
SHE'S NOT THERE."

(GIRL'S VOICE)
SOT: "SHE HAD A LOCKER UNDER
ME."

[Narration]
PHOTO/LOCKER   One she could reach. Britthany was just
four feet tall.
Paige could JUMP higher than that.

(COLBY)
SOT: "SHE HAD GOOD FORM."

(DOTSON)
SOT: "SHE COULD FAKE YOU OUT?"

(COLBY)
SOT: "UH-HUH... (BOYS NOD)"

(DOTSON)
SOT: "YOU ADMIT THAT TO ME?"

(COLBY)
SOT: "UH-HUH..."

(DOTSON)
SOT: "WOW!"

DANCE PHOTO

(HOLLY)
SOT: "SHE GAVE ME A PICTURE OF
HER. ONE OF THE PICTURES THAT
SHE HAD."

[Narration]
Holly Montgomery and Natalie Brooks
vowed to be Best Friends Forever.

(HOLLY)
SOT: "SHE GAVE ME A MAKEUP BAG"

[Narration]
For her birthday ... the SAME day Natalie
died.

TWO BOYS LAUGHING AND TALKING
ABOUT HAVING A CRUSH ON NATALIE
WHILE THE GIRLS EGG THEM ON

(MICHAEL)
SOT: "SHE HAD THE MOST BEAUTIFUL
EYES. I KINDA HAD A CRUSH ON HER."

(GIRLS "OOOH")

(COLBY)
SOT: "ALMOST EVERYBODY IN
SCHOOL DID!"

(DOTSON)
SOT: "WAIT A MINUTE, THE TWO OF
YOU BOTH HAD A CRUSH ON
NATALIE?"

(GIRLS SHOUT—"COLBY ADMIT IT
NOW. ADMIT IT!")

(COLBY)
SOT: "YEAH"

(GIRLS SQUEAL WITH DELIGHT!)

(HOLLY)
SOT: "MICHAEL?"

(MICHAEL)
SOT: "WHAT?"

(HOLLY)
SOT: "COME ON, ADMIT IT!"

(COLBY)
SOT: (EXASPERATED) "OK!"

(LAUGHTER)

[Narration]
These are kids who could make the faces
on Mount Rushmore grin.
But THEY think bullets got the best of
them.

(HOLLY)
SOT: "THEY STAYED ON THE 'A' AND 'B' HONOR ROLL ALL YEAR."

[Narration]
Stephanie thought she might like to be a nurse.
Natalie loved the stars.
Britthany always wanted to be Miss America.
Paige just wanted a trophy at this month's sports banquet.

(DOTSON)
SOT: "WHAT ARE YOU GOING TO MISS THE MOST ABOUT THESE FOUR PEOPLE?"

(MICHAEL)
SOT: "NATALIE'S SMILE ... PERSONALITY... ALWAYS LENDING A HELPING HAND."

(HOLLY)
SOT: "OUR SCHOOL WAS LIKE A CLOSE FAMILY ... LIKE BROTHERS AND SISTERS."

CLASSMATES LOOKING AT YEARBOOK AGAIN, FINALLY CLOSING THE BOOK

[Narration]
Our children are like library books, with a due date unknown.
These lives stopped at the start of their stories.
But their stories live on ... in friends who can tell them.
For Today ... Bob Dotson, NBC News, Jonesboro, Arkansas.

Where was the Non-Question/Question?

> (DOTSON)
> SOT: "WAIT A MINUTE, THE TWO OF
> YOU BOTH HAD A CRUSH ON
> NATALIE?"

That simple observation, not a question really, got every boy there to admit he had a crush on the dead girl. It was a bittersweet moment. Kids acting like kids again, instead of mourners.

WORKING FAST

That story was scripted in an hour. Under deadline. How do you write a longer story at the speed of spot news? This is how I do it:

Write the Middle of Your Story First

Don't sit in front of the computer screen and anguish over an opening line. The middle part of the story is the easiest place to start. It will be chock full of the facts that are right in your notebook. There is an added benefit to beginning in the middle. If the producer calls out, "You know that four minute piece you're working on? I really only have time for a minute fifty," you can cut without destroying the opening or the close.

How to Quickly Write a Good Opening Line

Often, when writing the middle of your story, the lead will suggest itself as you sort through your notes. But, if you are still at a loss for an opening line, here's another tip.

Look at the soundbites you've collected using the Rule of Threes, Filling the Silence and the Non-Question/Question. Do you have two good soundbites from the same person? You can use only one, so paraphrase the information in that second soundbite and make it your lead sentence.

A classmate of those little girls who were killed in Jonesboro showed me a school yearbook and said, "This will tell you about their lives." I decided not to use the soundbite, but it did give me an idea for an opening line:

"Sometimes the yearbook of life closes too soon."

We had pictures of students looking through that yearbook, so the line not only matched what we were showing, but it also set the story's emotional tone. When you paraphrase the second-best soundbite, you give your audience information that is central to your story and a compelling reason to stay tuned.

Don't Throw Away Thoughts

When soundbites prompt ideas, write them down. Carry an extra notebook in your back pocket. Those thoughts may not always fit your story, but don't throw them away. The next time you're pressed for an opening line, take out the notebook and start leafing through the ideas you have saved. One of them might prompt the perfect line.

Script #2: "Cave Rescue"

My "Ideas Notebook" has saved me many times. Once I was sent through the night to do a story about an explorer who was injured and trapped in the bottom of a cave. I had no chance to interview her rescuers. They were pulling the explorer from the earth when I arrived. Our live-shot location was twelve *miles* from the mouth of the cave. Fortunately, our editors in New York already had cut a core spot from videotape the rescuers brought with them to the surface.

During my flight to New Mexico, I talked constantly with the producers who were logging the tape. We determined there was a larger story to be told. Emily Mobley was injured in an unmapped part of that cave. Lost in the darkness. What would have happened to her without her friends, all of whom were world-class cavers? "Darkness" and "Friendship" seemed to be the keys to this story. I flipped through my Ideas Notebook reading every thought I'd ever jotted down about those two words. This is what I wrote on the plane ride to New Mexico:

"CAVE RESCUE" / NIGHTLY NEWS
CARLSBAD CAVERNS, NEW MEXICO
TOTAL RUNNING TIME 2:30
CORRESPONDENT: BOB DOTSON
PRODUCER: NED JUDGE

(DOTSON LIVE-OPEN)
Imagine slithering through a cave—a mile and a half long—climbing up a thousand foot maze dragging a broken leg. That's what it was like for Emily Mobley.

She had clawed her way beneath the earth for four days, after an eighty-pound boulder slipped and crushed her in the cave.

(TO TAPE CORE SPOT)

NATSOT:
Shadows chasing shadows.

NATSOT:
Now and then a whisper of sliding rope; the anxious, uneven breathing of sixty people lugging one of their own.

NATSOT:
Emily Mobley was at the bottom of one of the deepest caves in the United States—Letch-a-gee-yaha cavern—so big there were explorers at the opposite end that didn't even know the four-day rescue took place.

NATSOT:
The darkness would have been total for Mobley without her friends.

NATSOT:
They tugged her to the top an inch at a time. One and a half miles. In places they cushioned her weight with their own bodies and always kept a light for her to see above.

SOT: (INSERT MOBLEY FROM CAVE)
Mobley was mapping the cave, near Carlsbad, New Mexico, when a loose rock started this test of friendship.

NATSOT:
Pals came from all around the country. A cry of need seems to carry farther in darkness or perhaps we listen closer.

NATSOT:
They pulled her past places called Freakout and Nightmare and, finally, carried her out into the night, where the light above ...

(SHOW FULL MOON)

did not need batteries.

(TO DOTSON LIVE TAG LATEST INFO)

It struck me how quickly Mobley's friends had come to her rescue. That's why I wrote the line:

> A cry of need seems to carry farther in
> darkness or perhaps we listen closer.

FIND STRONG CENTRAL CHARACTERS

Look for strong central characters like Emily Mobley in every story you do. A few years ago, I was covering what I call a Grade C tornado. No deaths, no injuries, a mobile home smashed. The kind of natural disaster that leaves little to shoot.

Other reporters spent most of their time trailing after the mayor who said—predictably—"We need some assistance here."

Soundbites like that are quick, easy, sure things. But everyone gets the same bite.

You can do better. Let the mayor and your competitors go one way. You go another. Pick up official quotes from the wire services later. If they have substance, you can add them to your script.

My crew went around the corner and soon spotted a man in bib overalls searching through the remains of his mobile home. They introduced themselves. Began to visit as he continued to look. Another camera crew ran by, trying to find the mayor.

"What was the tornado like?" shouted the passing reporter.

"It sounded like a freight train," our guy mumbled.

That crew ran on. Mine stayed.

The man finally found what he was looking for.

Pictures?

No.

A big hunk of pink goo. He pulled it out of the muck, put it next to his face and smiled a toothless smile.

"Well, it got my teeth, but it didn't get me!"

Bingo! I had my close. Now, we could spend the next 20 minutes finding elements that would build to that close. No need to interview nineteen more people. We could weave the bib overall guy's search throughout the spot.

Everybody else went after those nineteen soundbites but gave scant time to the people who gave those quotes. The man in bib overalls became the thread that held together our entire piece.

Viewers relate to people, not soundbites. A strong central character helps them understand the story you have to tell.

FRED BENSON

The most successful man I ever met was Fred Benson. He has been a police chief, a fire chief, head of the rescue squad, baseball coach, teacher, builder and president of the Chamber of Commerce. Five times. At ninety he became a Rhode Island state driver's license examiner. If you're sixteen on Block Island and you want to drive, you've got to go see Fred.

He was eight when a farmer named Gurd Miliken took him in, and Fred still lives in the little room Gurd gave him, eighty-two years ago. Five generations of Milikens have grown up around him. They've repeatedly asked Fred to join them downstairs, where it is heated, but he refuses.

A few years back, Fred won the Rhode Island state lottery. Five hundred thousand dollars. He threw the biggest birthday party anyone can remember. Invited all the children on the island and announced he would pay the college tuition of any child who wanted to go.

Fred has always thought of his community first. A few years ago, there was a housing shortage on Block Island. So, at fifty-four, Fred went to college and got a degree. He wanted to teach high school shop. The island's four builders today all got their start with Fred.

Fred never married. Never had children of his own. But, for eighty-two years, he dedicated himself to the people of this island.

We were sitting one sunset watching waves crash against the rocky cliffs. I asked him, "Why?" Fred looked past the lighthouse to the waves breaking against the rocky cliff. Then turned and told me a story.

"When I was a little boy, the farmers used to meet for dinner on Saturday night. Each one would boast about his kids. Gurd Miliken had eight sons and me. I sat way down at the end of a long table." Fred paused to look at a pelican on a pole. "Gurd rose from his chair one night and pointed a long finger past all of his boys. He pointed right at me. 'You fellas wait and see what Fred Benson does. He'll be the best of 'em all.'"

Fred stopped talking for a long moment. Stared at the sunset for awhile. "I hope he knows how I turned out," he whispered. Then, more intensely, "I hope he knows how I turned out."

Fred Benson has found a safe harbor. Now he shows others the way. That's as good a description of what we storytellers do as any— show others the way. Help them see their choices. Perhaps avoid pitfalls.

SHOW THEM WHAT THEY MIGHT HAVE MISSED EVEN STANDING NEXT TO YOU

The best storytelling is filled with details. If you go into a kitchen and notice a bushel of green apples covered with dust, don't say, "We're standing here *live* in a kitchen." It's a kitchen with dusty apples. That image tells the viewer a lot more. Writers and photojournalists can help each other notice those details. On every assignment, take a few minutes. Back off. Compare notes. Make sure all of you are working on the same storyline. As the news changes, so may your outline. Constantly check in with each other. If flood waters thunder under a bridge, tell the reporter who has gone in search of victims. "The water sounds like a storm. Big trees floating past. Battering the bridge." The reporter may say, "Fine. Could be the opening to our story. One of the flood victims disappeared there." Keep comparing notes and you won't end up back at the uplink truck or edit room with two different stories.

Write to the Corners of Your Picture

Open your eyes and ears—all your senses. Look for things that the audience cannot see or hear for themselves. I call this, "Writing to the Corners of Your Picture." Don't waste time pointing out the obvious. Tell viewers what they might have missed even standing next to you. For instance, a huge tornado blows through a pine forest. You notice the smell driving through at dawn. Later, in editing, you remember that at the time you were trying to figure out how big the storm was. So, write:

> *"You could smell this storm's path before you could see it. A forest of torn trees, half a mile wide and 20 miles long."*

Writing to the corners of your picture adds meaning and context to this story. It gives the viewer more reasons to care.

Script #3: "Ruby Bridges"

I got a note from an assignment editor the other day. All it said was, "Go do a piece about Ruby Bridges. She's a civil rights activist who's now teaching kids." Well, I'd never heard of Ruby Bridges, but I suspected I already knew what she had to say. The struggle for civil rights is a familiar story. How could I get an audience to listen one more time? I found out the key was to remind viewers what it's like be six:

"RUBY BRIDGES" / TODAY SHOWSIDE
NEW ORLEANS, LOUISIANA
TOTAL RUNNING TIME 3:00
CORRESPONDENT: BOB DOTSON
PRODUCER: AMY WASSER-
                      STROM

[KATIE COURIC]
THOUGH YOU MAY NOT RECOGNIZE
HER NAME, YOU'VE PROBABLY SEEN
A PORTRAIT OF HOW RUBY BRIDGES
LOOKED ALMOST FORTY YEARS AGO
... AND AS NBC'S BOB DOTSON TELLS
US, YOU'LL WANT TO HEAR HER
STORY.

(TO SOT)

[RUBY BRIDGES DROPS INTO FRAME
AND PEERS OUT A DUSTY WINDOW.
SHE WATCHES CHILDREN ON
PLAYGROUND, AS CAMERA SLOWLY
ZOOMS INTO HER FACE]

NATSOT:
"OUR TOWN" BY AARON COPELAND
LONDON SYMPHONY ORCHESTRA
CBS MASTERWORKS, CUT 1

Ruby Bridges is back in a classroom that
once

[CHILDREN WALKING THROUGH
SUNBURST INTO SCHOOLYARD]

... was her prison.

[RUBY BRIDGES INTERVIEW]
"I REMEMBER STARING OUT OF THE
WINDOW BECAUSE IT LOOKED RIGHT
OVER THE PLAYGROUND, THIS
'HUGE' PLAYGROUND
(MOTIONS TO TINY PLAY AREA
BEHIND SCHOOL) ...

[CHILDREN PLAYING ON FRANTZ
SCHOOL PLAYGROUND LOW ANGLE
RUBY STARING OUT AT THEM]

[CHILDREN RUNNING THROUGH
SUNBURST, PAST CHAIN LINK FENCE,
INTO SCHOOLYARD]

THAT I WAS NEVER ALLOWED TO GO
OUT AND PLAY ON."

[SLOW DISSOLVE TO BLACK AND
WHITE FILM FROM 1960—CROWD
CHANTING]

[MOB CHANTING]
"TWO, FOUR, SIX, EIGHT, WE DON'T
WANT TO INTEGRATE..."

Because ... she wouldn't have been safe.

[BLACK AND WHITE FILM FROM
1960—WAVING REBEL FLAG]

In the fall of 1960 ... there was a mob out
there.

[RUBY BRIDGES INTERVIEW]
"THEY WERE SHOUTING AND
POINTING AND I DIDN'T QUITE
UNDERSTAND WHY THEY WERE SO
ANGRY."

[SLOW DISSOLVE TO PIX OF RUBY
BRIDGES AS YOUNG GIRL]

Ruby was just six...

[BLACK AND WHITE FILM FROM1960—
RUBY ENTERING SCHOOL]

NATURAL SOUND

Chosen to desegregate this New Orleans
school ... alone.

[BLACK AND WHITE FILM FROM
1960—ANXIOUS BLACK MAN LOOKING
AT SCHOOL, HE IS SURROUNDED BY
SEA OF WHITE FACES]

[RUBY BRIDGES INTERVIEW]
"WHEN I FIRST DROVE UP TO THE
SCHOOL, I ACTUALLY THOUGHT IT
WAS MARDI GRAS. YOU KNOW,
LIVING HERE IN NEW ORLEANS. THE
CROWD OUTSIDE. AND THEY WERE
BARRICADED. AND THEY WERE
THROWING THINGS. I KINDA FELT
LIKE I WAS IN THE MIDDLE OF A
PARADE."

[MORE BLACK AND WHITE FILM OF
RUBY ENTERING SCHOOL OR LAST
PAGE REAR-ANGLE VIEW OF RUBY
TRUDGING ALONG WITH HER LUNCH
BOX FROM BOOK]

The youngest soldier in the struggle for
civil rights.

[PAINTING FROM BOOK OF RUBY,
SITTING AT HER CLASSROOM DESK]

She went to her classroom...

[RUBY BRIDGES INTERVIEW]
"AND IT WAS EMPTY. SO MY FIRST
THOUGHT WAS, 'I'M TOO EARLY!'
(LAUGH)"

[BLACK AND WHITE FILM OF FATHER
OUTSIDE THE SCHOOL RAISING HIS
CHILD'S HANDS TO THE CROWD,
SHOWING THAT THEY WERE GOING
HOME]

All the OTHER parents had taken their
children home.

[PAINTINGS FROM BOOK—TEACHER
AND RUBY]

[BLACK AND WHITE FILM FROM1960—
WHITE CHILDREN RETURNING TO
SCHOOL PAST CROWD]

[RUBY BRIDGES INTERVIEW]
"AND THERE WERE NO KIDS THERE.
JUST ALL THESE EMPTY DESKS. AND
THAT STAYED THAT WAY THE WHOLE
YEAR."

[DOTSON QUESTION]
"DOES THIS HALLWAY BRING BACK
LONELY MEMORIES?"

[RUBY BRIDGES INTERVIEW]
"I WAS NEVER ALLOWED TO WALK
THESE HALLS. ONCE I GOT IN THE
CLASSROOM, THAT'S WHERE I
STAYED."

With her teacher, but Ruby never missed
a day.

Gradually, other kids DID come back.

[RUBY BRIDGES INTERVIEW]
"I WOULD SAY TO MY TEACHER, 'I
HEAR CHILDREN.'"

"AND THEN ONE DAY SHE OPENED
THIS DOOR AND THAT LED FROM THE
COAT CLOSET INTO THIS ROOM."

"THERE WERE FIVE OR SIX WHITE
KIDS ... AND I THOUGHT, 'OH, MY GOD.
LOOK AT THIS.' I FELT LIKE I HAD JUST
STEPPED INTO DISNEY WORLD."

[BLACK AND WHITE FILM FROM 1960—
WHITE DEMONSTRATOR ARRESTED]

[STANDUP COPY BEGINS]
"THE CURSES AND CROWDS FINALLY
FADED AWAY, BUT RUBY'S FAMILY
HAD PAID A TERRIBLE PRICE. HER
FATHER LOST HIS JOB. HER PARENTS
DIVORCED. RUBY STEPPED INTO
HISTORY'S SHADOW.

DOTSON WALKING IN
NEIGHBORHOOD NEXT TO SCHOOL

SUPER: BOB DOTSON
       NBC NEWS
       NEW ORLEANS

[STANDUP COPY CONTINUES VOICE
OVER]
"... RUBY STEPPED BACK INTO THE
SPOTLIGHT, DETERMINED TO HELP
OTHER CHILDREN WHO HAVE
PROBLEMS."
[END OF STANDUP COPY]

[CROSSING GUARD WHISTLING]

[ECU OF SCHOOL STOP SIGN]

[WIDE SHOT OF RUBY ENTERING
SCHOOL TODAY, WITH A GROUP OF
SIX-YEAR-OLDS]

[RUBY BRIDGES INTERVIEW]
"I THINK IT'S IMPORTANT THAT WE
BECOME MOTHER AND FATHER TO
EVERY CHILD."

SHE began with the children in HER old
school—Frantz Elementary.

[RUBY READING TO A GROUP OF SIX
YEAR OLDS]

[RUBY BRIDGES ASKS TWO BLACK
BOYS, ONE A BIT LIGHTER SKINNED
THAN THE OTHER]
"IT SHOULDN'T MATTER THAT GERALD
IS NOT THE SAME COLOR AS YOU?"

[BOY]
"NO, WE'RE STILL FRIENDS."

Ruby Bridges was too young to be bitter the first time she was here. Too wise to be bitter today.

[RUBY BRIDGES INTERVIEW]
"WE HAVE TO SPEND A LOT MORE TIME WITH OUR KIDS, MAKING SURE THAT THEY ARE NOT FACED WITH THOSE SAME THINGS THAT THIS SIX-YEAR-OLD WAS FACED WITH."

[NORMAN ROCKWELL PAINTING—A LITTLE GIRL IN WHITE STARCHED DRESS WALKS BENEATH A SCRAWLED CURSE, A CRUSHED TOMATO AT HER FEET, FEDERAL MARSHALS SURROUND HER. ONE WITH A COURT ORDER IN HIS POCKET]

NATSOT:
"OUR TOWN" BY AARON COPELAND LONDON SYMPHONY ORCHESTRA CBS MASTERWORKS, CUT 1

Ruby Bridges' proud march inspired Norman Rockwell's most powerful painting.
He called it "The Problem We All Live With..."

[RUBY HUGGING A GROUP OF SIX-YEAR-OLDS]

This little girl of six was able to do what she did because her heart and mind were wide open. Ruby's mission—today—is to keep other hearts and minds from closing.

"MAKE SURE YOU TELL SOMEBODY ABOUT THE STORY."

[RUBY TALKING TO CHILD ON HER KNEE]

For Today, Bob Dotson, NBC News, New Orleans.

I'm Sorry This Story Is So Long—I Didn't Have Time to Write a Short One

The long-form feature or magazine piece requires a structure far different from the short news story. You must use all the tools of a good novelist:

- Scene setting
- Foreshadowing
- Conflict
- Character growth
- Resolution

Let's take them one at a time.

Scene Setting

We knew that Ruby would want to see the classroom "that once was her prison." I discussed this with the camera crew. We decided they would go in ahead of her and use minimal lighting, so as not to distract from the moment. Ruby's old classroom had not changed much in forty years. It still had the tall windows where she had watched the screaming mobs. We figured that's where she would go first—to look out and remember.

Cameraman Rob Kane chose a wide-angle lens for this shot, the better to set the scene. Soundman Corky Gibbons placed a microphone near the bottom of the classroom door to record the click when Ruby entered and her footsteps echoed across the floor. He already had put a wireless microphone on Ruby when they first met, the better to record any quiet comments she might make as she wandered the room.

We were looking for a four-shot sequence:

1. Wide shot of the classroom
2. Tight shot of her feet

3. Over-the-shoulder shot as she looked out the window

4. Low-angle shot of her face.

Three of those shots would be easy to get in sequence—wide, over-the-shoulder and face—but the cut-in shot of the feet would have to come later. The camera could not be in two places at once. That feet shot would be important to help us edit. Cutting to the close-up can shorten the time it took Ruby to walk from the door to the window. How did we get that shot? Rob waited until Ruby started looking around the room again, then put his camera down at floor level and moved it until her feet were walking right to left in his view finder, the same direction she had been walking in the wide shot.

That four-shot sequence allowed us to introduce the black-and-white historical footage in context. As Ruby looked out the window at the children below, we half-dissolved to the old film, framed in the window. Our scene-setter uses all the television tools:

- *Natural sound*: Door click and footsteps
- *Narration*: "Ruby Bridges is back in a classroom that once was her prison..."
- *Picture*: Old classroom virtually unchanged
- *Graphics*: Black-and-white film of Ruby's ordeal framed in picture window
- *Editing*: Four shots to build pace into the opening

Foreshadowing

We give a hint of what's to come early in this story—the first line and opening soundbite:

Ruby Bridges is back in a classroom that once

... was her prison.

> [RUBY BRIDGES INTERVIEW]
> "I REMEMBER STARING OUT OF THE
> WINDOW BECAUSE IT LOOKED RIGHT
> OVER THE PLAYGROUND [...] THAT I
> WAS NEVER ALLOWED TO GO OUT
> AND PLAY ON."

The picture reinforces the foreshadowing. The classroom's tall, wooden windows—lit in silhouette—resemble jail-cell bars. All this sets up a bit of a mystery. It tempts the audience to find out more.

Conflict

The essence of storytelling is conflict. Something has to be resolved. Ruby faces a mob. Her parents divorce. Her father loses his job. Conflict aplenty here.

Character Growth

The key to good storytelling is how that conflict changes the characters in your story. They must learn something. At first Ruby seemed unaffected.

> She went to her classroom ...

> [RUBY BRIDGES INTERVIEW]
> "AND IT WAS EMPTY. SO MY FIRST
> THOUGHT WAS, 'I'M TOO EARLY!'
> (LAUGH)"

Ruby saw the world through six-year-old eyes. When her father was tossed off the job and her parents' marriage broke up, she was content to step into history's shadow. That changes after her brother was murdered near their old school...

> "... RUBY STEPPED BACK INTO THE
> SPOTLIGHT, DETERMINED TO HELP

OTHER CHILDREN WHO HAVE
PROBLEMS."

Resolution

Ruby returns to Frantz Elementary, this time as a teacher her-
self:

[RUBY BRIDGES INTERVIEW]
"WE HAVE TO SPEND A LOT MORE
TIME WITH OUR KIDS, MAKING SURE
THAT THEY ARE NOT FACED WITH
THOSE SAME THINGS THAT THIS SIX-
YEAR-OLD WAS FACED WITH."

The conflict is resolved. Ruby now understands that her role in
history is not finished. That sets up the final thought which summa-
rizes the point of the story:

This little girl of six was able to do what
she did because her heart and mind were
wide open. Ruby's mission—today—is to
keep other hearts and minds from
closing.

PUT STORIES INTO CONTEXT

We all know what is and what ought to be. Many of us don't
know what was. Journalists must add that context to every story. With
Ruby Bridges, I considered showing the famous Norman Rockwell
painting first, then telling her story, but concluded that viewers would
start thinking about the painting. Ruby Bridges is the story, not
Norman Rockwell. We had to carefully construct an emotional outline
that would make people care more about her.

First, we showed the audience that Ruby has a great sense of humor. She's engaging, lovely. This humor softens the tragic story we have to tell. Makes Ruby seem less like a civil rights icon, more like a neighbor. Her humor invited the audience to listen. Then, we could tell them what she endured—a six-year-old, marching through hateful crowds—day after day. Everyone's been six, so viewers understand how terrible that would be. Next, we tossed in a comic soundbite to lighten the mood. Unrelenting sorrow turns viewers away.

> [RUBY BRIDGES INTERVIEW]
> "WHEN I FIRST DROVE UP TO THE SCHOOL, I ACTUALLY THOUGHT IT WAS MARDI GRAS. YOU KNOW, LIVING HERE IN NEW ORLEANS. THE CROWD OUTSIDE. AND THEY WERE BARRICADED. AND THEY WERE THROWING THINGS. I KINDA FELT LIKE I WAS IN THE MIDDLE OF A PARADE."

After that, we could return to serious matters. Here, we shifted the point of view from a child's perspective to a parent's. Told the viewer about the sacrifices Ruby's mother and father made. By now the viewer knows most of Ruby's story. We've shown her ordeal through a child's eyes and a parent's perspective. Both universal elements that touch viewers deeply. Only then do we introduce the famous Normal Rockwell picture. The audience may say, "Oh, yeah, I remember that." But the painting, placed here, doesn't overpower Ruby's story. Viewers are already caught up in it and want to know more.

We ended with a twist to make a point. The audience might expect Ruby to make a final plea for tolerance between blacks and whites. Instead, the two little boys she picked to illustrate the need for tolerance are both African-American.

[RUBY BRIDGES ASKS TWO BLACK
BOYS, ONE A BIT LIGHTER SKINNED
THAN THE OTHER]
"IT SHOULDN'T MATTER THAT GERALD
IS NOT THE SAME COLOR AS YOU?"

[BOY]
"NO, WE'RE STILL FRIENDS."

That's the essence of Ruby's message. Skin color—regardless of color—should make no difference. The visual surprise helped to drive home that point in a way the audience was not expecting. In other words, I *wrote to the corners of the picture*, adding details that the audience might miss.

Section
Two

MSNBC, Fox, CNN—all do a good job of processing raw information, but you don't have to be a journalist to find that information anymore. Anyone can look it up on the Internet. For our profession to survive, we must bring context and understanding to the viewer. We must become better storytellers.

The main reason we tell anyone anything is to elicit a response, to see how he or she reacts. Storytelling begins with how the news affects the *viewers*, not the people we cover. Look for the compelling emotion. Will it make them angry? Happy? Sad? Build upon that central emotion, not with florid writing, but with strong images.

Great stories are like onions. No, not because they make you cry. They have many layers. They communicate on many levels. They are laced with things that make them widely appealing. On the surface is the tale you must tell, but under that a series of strong images and sounds—picture and audio designed to help the viewer *experience* the story, not just learn about it.

We work in the last mass medium. You don't need a Ph.D. to turn on TV, but some viewers have one. Craft your reports in such a way so as not to insult the intelligence of people who know your subject, but, at the same time, try to make your story fascinating for everyone else. Some will watch because they like your pictures; others because they are interested in the subject. Whatever. Highlight the universal elements—love and hate; happiness and sadness—emotions that interest the broadest group of viewers.

Script #4: "Pearl Harbor's Untold Story"

This piece tells a story half a century old. Look for the universal elements that make it seem as urgent as today's headlines:

"PEARL HARBOR'S UNTOLD STORY" /
TODAY SHOWSIDE
PEARL HARBOR, HAWAII
TOTAL RUNNING TIME 5:56
CORRESPONDENT: BOB DOTSON
PRODUCER: DAVE RIGGS

[LEAD INFORMATION]
I LOVE A YARN WITH AN O. HENRY
TWIST AT THE END, THE KIND WHERE
PAUL HARVEY PAUSES, THEN SAYS,
"NOW YOU KNOW THE REST OF THE
STORY..." THIS ONE'S A DOOZY.

DURING WORLD WAR TWO,
JAPANESE-AMERICANS WERE NOT
THE ONLY VICTIMS OF WARTIME
HYSTERIA. IN HAWAII, GERMANS,
ITALIANS, AUSTRIANS, FINNS AND
NORWEGIANS—RESIDENT ALIENS
AND NATURALIZED AMERICAN
CITIZENS—WERE ALSO ROUNDED UP
AND THROWN INTO INTERNMENT
CAMPS.

THE SMOKE HAD NOT YET DRIFTED
AWAY FROM THE JAPANESE SNEAK
ATTACK AT PEARL HARBOR BEFORE
THE ARRESTS BEGAN. A DAY LATER
112 EUROPEANS AND EUROPEAN-
AMERICANS WERE IN CUSTODY.
MORE FOLLOWED.

THEY WERE HERDED ONTO A SPIT OF
SAND AT THE ENTRANCE OF
HONOLULU HARBOR. IMMIGRANTS
HAD BEEN QUARANTINED THERE IN
THE 19TH CENTURY. THIS "ELLIS
ISLAND" OF THE PACIFIC BECAME
THEIR PRISON.

IN THE EARLY DAYS THEY WERE
ALLOWED NO NEWSPAPERS OR
MAGAZINES. TO KEEP MENTALLY
ACTIVE, THEY FORMED "THE
UNIVERSITY OF SAND ISLAND." THIS
WAS NO ORDINARY GROUP. ONE MAN
KNEW BY HEART NINE OF ANTON
BRUCKNER'S SYMPHONIES. HE
COULD HUM AND ANALYZE EACH
ONE. A VIOLINIST FROM GERMANY
AND A COMPOSER FROM NORWAY
ADDED THEIR KNOWLEDGE.
ANOTHER TAUGHT CITY PLANNING.
SOME GAVE TALKS ON HUMAN
ANATOMY, HISTORY, RELIGION AND
ASTRONOMY. DURING THE
BLACKOUTS AT NIGHT, THE GROUP
SPENT MANY EVENINGS
STARGAZING.

THEIR DETENTION WAS MADE
POSSIBLE BECAUSE HABEAS
CORPUS HAD BEEN SUSPENDED ON
THE ISLANDS. SECRETARY OF WAR
HENRY L. STIMSON WROTE IN HIS
DIARY THAT THE MILITARY COULD
KEEP AMERICAN CITIZENS IN
CUSTODY BECAUSE "HAWAII IS
UNDER A STATE OF MARTIAL LAW
AND ... WE CAN DO WHAT WE PLEASE
WITH THEM."

AFTER THE WAR, GENERAL DELOS C. EMMONS, ONE OF THE MILITARY GOVERNORS, STATED: "UNDOUBTEDLY, MISTAKES WERE MADE." BUT NO APOLOGIES WERE EVER GIVEN. THOSE WHO WERE INTERNED SELDOM SPOKE OF THEIR TIME IN THE CAMP. THEY WENT ON TO LIVE REMARKABLE, AMAZINGLY PATRIOTIC LIVES, AS YOU WILL SEE.

ONLY A FEW ARE LEFT WHO CAN TELL THE STORY OF WHAT HAPPENED.

=-=-=-=-=-=-=-=-script-=-=-=-=-=-=-=

THE RED BALL OF SUNRISE FILLS THE SCREEN	It was a sunrise of fire ... and the memory still burns.
	NATSOT BOMBING
JAPANESE ZEROES APPEAR. THE DESTRUCTION OF PEARL HARBOR BEGINS	These sizzling seas sent the United States into World War Two ... half a century ago ... this year.
	NATSOT BOMBING
RED SUNLIGHT REFLECTED IN THE HARBOR	Before the memory of that day bled away 110 thousand people were arrested in America for what another country did.
AUTHORITIES BEGIN ARRESTING PEOPLE	
	NATSOT VINTAGE MUSIC

PEOPLE ROUSTED FROM HOMES, BUSINESSES AND PLACED BEHIND BARBED WIRE	They were plucked from homes and businesses and penned behind barbed wire. Most looked like the Japanese who attacked Pearl Harbor. But in Hawaii they rounded up Italian Americans too.
DISSOLVE TO JOE PACIFIC SUPER: JOE PACIFIC (0:55–1:01)	"THIS MAN CAME DOWN, SHOWED ME A BADGE. HE SAY 'JOE, I GOTTA TAKE YOU DOWN TO POLICE, UH, IMMIGRATION TO CHECK YOUR PAPERS.' I SAYS TO HIM, 'WAIT FIVE MINUTES I MAKE A SANDWICH FOR MY DAUGHTER AND FOR MYSELF.' HE SAYS, 'NAW, YOU DON'T HAVE TO DO THAT BECAUSE YOU'LL BE BACK IN FIFTEEN MINUTES.'"
STILL PIX—JOE AND DAUGHTER	Joe Pacific was gone 4 months. "AND THEY LEFT MY DAUGHTER ALONE ... IN THAT HOUSE ... ALL ALONE. SHE WAS THERE FOR THREE DAYS ... ALONE."
STILL PIX—PREIS' BW AFTERMATH FILM	Alfred Preis and his wife, Jana, were picked up ... in the first long breath after the bombs.
ALFRED PREIS SPEAKING	"WE WENT AND WERE BROUGHT DOWN IN A DARKENED CITY AT SNAKE PACE. DEAD SILENT, INTERRUPTED BY SHOTS FROM TIME TO TIME."

HONOLULU IMMIGRATION HEADQUARTERS	Honolulu Immigration Headquarters ... They thought they were needed as translators ... Austrians who could speak several languages.
ALFRED PREIS SPEAKING DOTSON CUTAWAY	"(MY WIFE) WAS TAKEN AWAY AND I NEVER SAW HER FOR A LONG TIME. I FELT A COLD SHARP OBJECT IN MY BACK. AND (A VOICE) SAID, 'GO AHEAD NOW.' UNTIL I CAME TO A STEEL LADDER OR STAIRWAY AND HE PUSHED ME UP WITH A BAYONET. I OPENED THE DOOR MYSELF AND FOUND LITTLE GLOWING SPOTS IN ALL DIFFERENT HEIGHTS. THESE WERE BUNK ROOMS AND THERE WERE PEOPLE ON ALL LAYERS OF THE BUNKS AND THEY WERE SMOKING CIGARETTES."
STILL PIX—CONDUCTOR/CHEFS AND PAN OF OTTO'S ORENSTEIN'S PASSPORT	The former conductor of the Honolulu symphony was there. So were most of the chefs of the Hawaii's great hotels. Even a Jew from Vienna who had escaped a Nazi concentration camp.
OTTO ORENSTEIN SPEAKING	"I THOUGHT IT WAS A RATHER UNJUST THING THAT FIRST THE GERMANS WOULD INTERN ME, THEN THE BELGIANS WOULD INTERN ME, NOW THE AMERICANS DOING IT TOO. WHAT DID I DO?"
WS DOTSON/ORENSTEIN ON SAND ISLAND WITH HONOLULU IN BACKGROUND	Otto Orenstein had the misfortune of speaking with a German accent.

ALFRED PREIS SPEAKING	"A MAN IN UNIFORM DEMANDED WE EMPTY OUR POCKETS AGAIN. EVEN TOOK OUR WEDDING RINGS AWAY BECAUSE HE WAS AFRAID WE'D USE THEM TO BRIBE SOMEBODY."
STILL PIX ALFRED AND JANA AS NEWLYWEDS	Alfred Preis was a newlywed.
ALFRED PREIS SPEAKING	"WHEN THEY TOOK THE WEDDING RING AWAY FROM ME I BROKE DOWN BECAUSE WHAT WENT THROUGH MY MIND—NOT EVEN NAZIS WOULD HAVE DONE THAT."
ORENSTEIN WALKS WITH WIFE	NATSOT SHOWING WIFE WHERE OLD CAMP WAS
STILL PIX—CAMP	Only a few are left who can tell the story ... an address list of long-forgotten names.
	NATSOT "BARBED WIRE WAS THERE."
DISSOLVE TO ALFRED PREIS SPEAKING	They were herded onto Sand island in the harbor across from Honolulu ... with immigrants from Finland and Norway as well.
	"NO FLOORS. COTS WITHOUT MATTRESSES. MUD ON THE GROUND. SO WE LIED ON THE COTS AND THE COTS STARTED TO SINK AND SINK AND SINK AND SINK. WE—VIRTUALLY THE FIRST MANY NIGHTS—SLEPT ON THE MUD."

	[STANDUP COPY]
SETTING SUN OVER TOWER	THE CAMP GOT SO CROWDED, SOME PEOPLE WERE TRANSFERRED TO DETENTION CENTERS ON THE

SUPER: BOB DOTSON
       HONOLULU, HAWAII
       (4:34–4:41)
	MAINLAND. WHEN THEY POINTED OUT THAT FEW OTHER ITALIAN AMERICANS OR AUSTRIAN AMERICANS WERE BEING HELD, THEY WERE RELEASED. BUT SOLDIERS MET THEM AT THE GATE, TRANSPORTED THEM BACK TO HAWAII AND LOCKED THEM UP AGAIN. DURING THE WAR, THE ISLANDS WERE UNDER MILITARY RULE,SO IT WAS ALL PERFECTLY LEGAL.

JOE PACIFIC SPEAKING	"FROM SAND ISLAND I COULD SEE MY HOUSE ... "
STILL PIX SHOE STORE	By the time Joe Pacific was released, someone had stolen all the shoes in his store.
JOE PACIFIC SPEAKING	"SO CLOSE AND SO FAR."
ALFRED PREIS AT DRAFTING TABLE	Alfred Preis could not find work as an architect. The Orensteins lost their home.
DOTSON SPEAKING TO ORENSTEIN	"DID ANYONE EVERY APOLOGIZE?"
OTTO ORENSTEIN SPEAKING	"NOPE, NOBODY PAID ME 20 THOUSAND DOLLARS EITHER."
JAPANESE-AMERICANS IN CAMPS	As the government did for Japanese-Americans who were sent to such camps.
DISSOLVE TO AMERICAN FLAG AND THE THREE FACES OF ORENSTEIN, PREIS AND PACIFIC	Yet these three—with hearts shot full of pain—continue to love America.

PREIS ON BOAT HEADING OUT TO ARIZONA MEMORIAL	NATSOT BOAT AND FLAG RAISING CEREMONY
	Preis ... in particular ... set out to reclaim his patriotism. Not far from his island prison, he offered a simple tribute to those who fell at Pearl Harbor. He is the architect who designed the U.S.S. Arizona memorial.
HE IS SURROUNDED BY SAILORS WHO HAVE COME BEFORE THE TOURISTS THIS MORNING FOR A RE-ENLISTMENT CEREMONY.	NATSOT SAILOR THANKS PREIS His life ... like that war ... found victory in defeat.
ONE OF THEM RECOGNIZES PREIS AND THANKS HIM FOR CREATING SUCH A TOUCHING MEMORIAL	NATSOT For Today, Bob Dotson, NBC News, Pearl Harbor.
FINALLY, HE IS LEFT ALONE WITH HIS THOUGHTS	

How does this story make you feel? Sad?

OTTO ORENSTEIN SPEAKING

"I THOUGHT IT WAS A RATHER UNJUST THING THAT FIRST THE GERMANS WOULD INTERN ME, THEN THE BELGIANS WOULD INTERN ME, NOW THE AMERICANS DOING IT TOO.

WHAT DID I DO?"

Mad?

ALFRED PREIS SPEAKING

"WHEN THEY TOOK THE WEDDING RING AWAY FROM ME I BROKE DOWN

BECAUSE WHAT WENT THRU MY
MIND—NOT EVEN NAZIS WOULD
HAVE DONE THAT."

Notice, we highlighted these emotions to set up the final amazing surprise. Preis so loved his adopted country, even after all he had been through, that he designed one of its most famous memorials.

A compelling story needs to emphasize one other universal element—*hope*. Without hope, audiences tune out. We also run the risk of turning people away if we fail to put things into context. Don't overwhelm viewers with information. To survive, we must help them sort through that information, help them understand.

IT'S TV, FOLKS, NOT THE MOVIES

Remember, people normally don't watch TV news in a darkened room. They're brushing their teeth, eating breakfast, getting kids off to school; they are cooking dinner, answering the phone, picking up toys. Your task is to get them to pay attention to your story.

How to Defeat the TV Remote Control

My first writing teacher, Fred Shook, told me that clarity and accuracy create the foundation of all good news stories. You must write to express, not impress. People want something from your writing. Happiness. Understanding. Insight. An old woman watching a home movie isn't just seeing pictures of her family, "She sees her father walk through the scenes of her childhood. No longer just dead 47 years." Write to create imagery. Look for little details that can be metaphors for what's happening at a level the viewer cannot see. What image does this line create?

"Each morning as the sun slips over the horizon, the paint pot tips and spills, casting its beauty on the people below."

Metaphors can help you instill grace in your writing and provide a bit of dramatic tension.

"Race day dawned still and clear, as if the sky had intended to hold its breath."

Another effective way to create vivid imagery—personalize what you write.

"A friend of mine played football for a school so small that the players changed uniforms at half time and came back as the band."

Also, pay attention to the sound of your writing.

"Yellowstone in winter is a world of fire and ice: a teakettle land of boiling steam and belly-deep snow."

Your ear is often the best copy editor you'll find.

"The Old West was America's forge, and the pioneers who passed through it had spirits of hammered steel."

Avoid weak, wimpy verbs. "Is" is the dullest verb in the language. Reach for words that say more, that do more, that enhance the copy. One time in Alaska, I covered a sled dog race "... on a day so cold, you could spit and watch it bounce."

Be Conversational

Write the way you speak. When I'm struggling to make something clear, I follow the advice of Roy Peter Clark of the Poynter Institute for Media Studies, and fantasize a conversation with my mom. As Mr. Clark puts it, if my mother asked me, "What did you learn at City Hall today?" which would I tell her:

- "The council agreed to support a project to aid small businesses by giving them low-interest loans."
- "Well, ma, small businesses are struggling, but the city council thinks it has found a way to help them out."

Gobbledygook and Clichés

Rid your stories of these verbal weeds. Gobbledygook confuses people who don't know official jargon. How many times have you heard firemen say a burning building is "fully involved?" What does that mean? Is the house having an affair? Also, weed out clichés. There is clarity in clichés, but they say something so succinctly we wear them out. If you can't think of a better image, try twisting the tired old line:

"A fellow by the name of John Colter was the first man to tell the world about Yellowstone. Nobody back east believed his fanciful tales of hot springs and boiling mud. People thought there might be a crystal heaven somewhere out west, but if there was a hell, they said, it was Colter's hell. Even today, few people have seen this great yellowstone land in winter when hell freezes over."

Active Voice

The single most important change you can make to improve your writing is to eliminate the passive voice. Write in the active voice.

Which creates the stronger image?

- "A lot of noise was made by the approaching hurricane..."

- "The hurricane thunders off shore..."

Writing in the active voice forces you to think about what is happening now. It produces tighter copy. More interesting stories. Audiences assign a greater sense of urgency to stories written in the active voice.

Write in Threes

Grouping things in threes also can make your writing memorable.

- "Red, white and blue"
- "Life, liberty and the pursuit of happiness"
- "Father, Son and Holy Ghost"

Each has a rhythm, a rhythmic pattern of threes.

Surprises

Build into every story a little surprise—an abrupt natural sound, unanticipated picture or an unsuspected turn in the script. Anything to rivet a viewer's attention. Surprises lure uninterested viewers to the screen, help viewers feel something about the story.

Say you're doing a market-basket report on the high cost of lemons. Find a little kid running a lemonade stand. Ask him, "Why should I buy your lemonade?" He might say, "Well, it's hot. It's good lemonade." But I remember such a story where a young boy looked at the camera and said, "Why should you buy my lemonade? It tastes pinkish."

Bingo! There's a surprise. In the middle of a financial story, you deliver a little moment of fun, a grace note that gives your report an emotional outline. Some reason for people to care.

How to Highlight a Story's Natural Drama

Don't overlook a story's natural drama. If you're covering the demolition of a building and cut to the explosion a split second before, that's not nearly as dramatic as when you build in a pause before the blast.

Often, when news producers tell us to tighten stories, we end up chopping everything, including the story's natural drama. Write tighter in other parts of your piece to save time for the drama to play itself out.

For example, if a hundred-year-old man hits a ball during a softball game and runs to first base, don't cut away to another shot. It's more dramatic to see—in real time—whether he can make it. Every good story should have a bit of drama. Stringing together facts is not enough.

HOW TO BECOME A STORYTELLER

A friend of mine used to moan, "I can't write." He's a photo-journalist. A wonderful storyteller with pictures, but words frighten him. He once covered an all-night concert. I went to pick up his tape.

"Anything going on?" I asked.

"Not much," he answered. "Breakfast was either smoked or passed around in a bottle."

I grinned. "Bet you got pictures of that."

"Yep."

"Well," I chuckled. "Thanks for my opening line,"

"Huh?"

"'Breakfast was either smoked or passed around in a bottle.' I think that kind of sums up this party, doesn't it?"

"Well..."

"Thanks," I said. "You're a helluva writer."

Whether your specialty is sound or picture or words, ultimately your task is the same as the guy who sat around a campfire two thousand years ago and told about his hunt. We're still trying to tell our stories in ways that people will want to hear them. So, don't get hung up on a job description. When people ask me what I do for a living, I say, "Storyteller."

Writing—good writing—is timeless.

One of the most powerful lines ever scribbled is as old as the Bible:

"Jesus wept."

Subject. Verb.

Not, "Jesus, a carpenter of Nazareth, age 30, was executed in the pre-dawn darkness..."

Just, "Jesus wept."

Tight writing like that is essential for our visual medium, which needs sentences strong enough to push the story along, but short enough to leave plenty of room for natural sound and pictures.

PICKING SOUNDBITES

How do you pick the best soundbites? Robert Frost used to say, "A poem begins as a lump in the throat." Look for soundbites that give you that lump in the throat. They should make you happy or sad, pleased or mad. But, they should stick in memory. When they do, write them down. Carry an extra notebook in your back pocket. Those soundbites may not always fit the story you're working on, but don't throw these thoughts away. The next time you're pressed for an idea, take out the notebook and start leafing through those ideas. One of them might prompt the perfect line.

THE GAME OF *WHAT IF?*

Here's another little mind game to help you work faster and more efficiently. As your story progresses, ask yourself, "If I had to leave right now, what would be my opening shot? My closing shot? What would be the point of this story?" During breaking news, those answers may change minute-by-minute and, of course, your story must change with them. That's the business you're in. You must make adjustments. But if you keep the end of your story clearly in sight, you can construct a path that will take your audience there. You won't waste time shooting pictures or interviews you won't need.

GETTING STARTED

You aren't ready to write a story until you can state in one sentence what you want the audience to learn from your report. You should be able to answer that in a complete sentence with subject, verb and object. "Outside money is altering the city's architecture," "This cow has never taken an order in her life." "You can't murder a pumpkin," etc. Prove the points visually. Very seldom will you state the point of your story verbally.

Pictures Come First

Pictures are powerful storytelling tools. "Write" them first. Think how the pictures should progress in your story. Remember, there is a language of video, just as there is of words. They must both flow—one to the other—logically and smoothly. Resist writing words first, then using picture to cover those words like wallpaper. That is rarely the most compelling way. If you are not personally shooting the pictures, ask the photojournalist, "What's the best picture you have to open the story? What's the most powerful picture for the close?" Then, build your script around these images.

Script #5: "Atlanta Bombing"

I arrived on the scene of an abortion clinic bombing in Atlanta one time after all the best pictures had been fed to an edit room. No photojournalist had shot more than a small portion of the story. So, I called the producer logging pictures and asked:

- What's your best picture?
- What moment gave you a lump in the throat?
- What main points of the story don't have picture?
- What's your best closing shot?

The answers to those four questions gave me what I needed to quickly script this live-shot core spot.

"ATLANTA BOMBING" / NIGHTLY NEWS
ATLANTA, GEORGIA
TOTAL RUNNING TIME 1:45
CORRESPONDENT: BOB DOTSON
PRODUCERS: VARIOUS

	The first explosion about 9:30 this morning blew out windows at the North Atlanta Family Planning Clinic.
	Ten people were in the building. Four in the first floor doctors' offices. No one was hurt.
EYEWITNESS	
	"It only lasted for a few seconds. They sounded like shots. You didn't know what was goin' on."
REPORTER	
	"Where were you in the building and where was the explosion..."
SECOND BOMB EXPLODES BEHIND WITNESS	(SECOND BOMB EXPLODES, WITNESS FLINCHES)
	"My God!"
	This second explosion about an hour later injured a television photographer, a federal agent and at least four others.
POLICE OFFICER	
	"Stand back! Get back! Get back! Let's go!"

That blast, felt for miles, tore through a dumpster on the other side of the building.

Additional security was dispatched to all Atlanta abortion clinics, while the bomb squad scoured the area for other explosive devices.

No one has claimed responsibility for these explosions. Police say there were no calls to 911 beforehand and clinic workers received no threats.

NURSE EYEWITNESS

"Our operating room and our recovery room are gone..."

REPORTER

"So, the bomb was inside the clinic?"

NURSE EYEWITNESS

"It was inside the clinic. Our whole clinic is gone."

This same clinic was bombed 13 years ago in a different Atlanta location. But authorities are not sure today's bombs were actually targeting the abortion offices.

FEDERAL AGENT

"As far as the motive, I know a lot of you are assuming this is related to abortion clinic violence. That is definitely a possibility, but we are not ruling out the possibility of domestic terrorism unrelated to clinic violence."

Agents would not reveal what kind of explosives were found, but say they will check first to see if this bombing is connected to the explosion at the Atlanta Olympics.

> (SIREN)
>
> Perhaps most troubling, police say, was the timing of today's explosions. The stronger of the two set to go off just after federal agents arrived.
>
> (BACK TO DOTSON LIVE TAG)

WHAT GOES IN THE MIDDLE?

In the main body of the story, concentrate on crafting three to five key points, which you support visually once you have identified them. Make them as clear and sharp as you can, so they'll cut through the clutter and stick in the viewer's memory.

Most of the time, the best place for a reporter to appear on camera is in the middle of the story. The standup gives the viewer information you can't visualize; information that transitions from one location to another. I know live shots generally begin and end with reporters on camera, but that often leads to weak formula reporting. The number of times a reporter appears on camera will never matter to viewers, if you don't tell them why this story is important to their lives.

Script #6: "The Boys of Winter"

Whenever possible, try to find a standup location that doesn't interrupt the flow of the story. I once did a piece about elderly softball players in St. Petersburg, Florida. Decided to tape my on-camera bridge from the stands during their game. Sat down next to some fans; explained what I had in mind, then, waited until someone got a hit, so the fans would be cheering and following the play, not staring at the camera.

We ended up with this:

"THE BOYS OF WINTER"/TODAY SHOW
ST. PETERSBURG, FLORIDA
TOTAL RUNNING TIME 4:00
CORRESPONDENT: BOB DOTSON
PRODUCER: BOB DOTSON

LINE OF OLD SOFTBALL PLAYERS
WHIP OFF THEIR BALL CAPS AND
RECITE THEIR CLUB'S CREED WHILE
THE CAMERA TRUCKS LEFT TO RIGHT
DOWN THEIR LINE OF FACES

[PLAYERS CHANTING CHEER]
"What's the matter with 75? We're the
boys who are still alive! Rah, Rah! 75!"
(Cheering)

BALL PLAYERS BEGIN TO WARM UP

These guys have been taken off time's
mailing list.

Pappy Hill...

[PLAYER]
"Okay, Pappy, right over the plate!"

Is pushing 80

OLD MAN GETS A HIT AND WOBBLES
TO FIRST BASE

Natural Sound: Hit and cheers

George Bakewell is 99.

[FAN SHOUTS]
"You get better and better, George!"

DOTSON ON CAMERA SITTING WITH   [DOTSON STANDUP]
CHEERING FANS   You know, if Babe Ruth were alive today,

SUPER: BOB DOTSON) NBC NEWS	he would be two years younger than George. (Fans Laugh)
	This is Bakewell's 25th season. And he still rarely strikes out.
BAKEWELL LEANS HIS FACE CLOSE TO A FEMALE FAN	[BAKEWELL KISSES FAN] "Watch this! (Smooch)"
SHE OBLIGINGLY KISSES HIM	
GEORGE'S NEW WIFE SHOWING PHOTO OF THEIR WEDDING TO FRIENDS IN STANDS. SHE AND GEORGE ARE LEAVING THE CHURCH UNDER AN HONOR GUARD OF CROSSED BATS	Perhaps it's because he recently got married and he went on his honeymoon in Switzerland, hiking.
GEORGE CLIMBING STAIRS IN HIS RETIREMENT HOME	[BAKEWELL] "(Singing) Let me call you sweetheart..."
	I've been trying to keep up with George for years.
GEORGE TIPS HIS CAP TO WOMAN IN HALLWAY AT TOP OF STAIRS	BAKEWELL] "Good morning."
	[WOMAN] "Hello, George."
JUMPING ROPE	At 87 he used to jump rope dozens of times a day just to keep his blood pumping.

GEORGE FLEXES HIS ARM AND POINTS TO MUSCLE	[BAKEWELL] "See that little egg?" (LAUGHTER)
WORKING OUT WITH IRON BAT	Now, he swings an eight-pound iron bat. [BAKEWELL] "Keeps the shoulders loose."
GEORGE RIDES STATIONARY BIKE NEXT TO A GROUP OF ELDERLY WOMEN WATCHING TV IN OLD FOLKS HOME	And rides a stationary bike 20 miles
GEORGE WAVES TO A WOMAN AS HE HOPS OFF BIKE AND RUNS OUT	[BAKEWELL] "See you later, Honey."
GEORGE'S GROUPIES, NO ONE UNDER 75, SIT IN THE BLEACHERS HE GOES FROM ONE TO THE NEXT GRABBING KISSES	A fellow like that naturally attracts a following.
WOMAN SMILES AFTER A KISS AND SAYS CONSPIRATORIALLY TO CAMERA	[WOMAN FAN] "The kissing bandit!"
FELLOW PLAYERS, OUT ON THE BASE PATHS, LOOK ENVIOUS	Some of the new guys would like to be in his cleats, but— [PLAYER] "I don't practice like he does. I smoke 14 cigars a day."

GEORGE SITTING IN STANDS WITH
HIS NEW BRIDE BONNIE

Fans don't bother his new bride Bonnie.

[BONNIE]
"Let him have them. I don't care. He's
mine. They're not going to get him."

GEORGE THROWN OUT AT FIRST
BASE. BONNIE APPLAUDS, THEN,
WONDERS WHAT HAPPENED, A
BEFUDDLED LOOK ON HER FACE.
GEORGE TELLS US

[BAKEWELL]
"She don't know anything about baseball,
yet. I was out by 50 feet!"

MACHINE RATTLING DOWN FIELD,
LAYING DOWN CHALK LINES

No matter, beyond this line is an endless
summer.

TEAMS CHOOSING UP SIDES

These two teams, the Kids and the Cubs
have stood together three days a week
and 60 games a season for 62 years.

OLD MAN HITS HOME RUN
SCOREKEEPER CREAKS OUT OF HIS
FOLDING CHAIR AND TODDLES TO
SCOREBOARD TO CHANGE THE
SCORE
THE HITTER CROSSES HOME PLATE
BEFORE THE SCOREKEEPER IS DONE

Some have been known to circle the
bases faster than the scorekeeper could
keep score.

GEORGE PAUSES LEANING AGAINST
THE DUGOUT

[BAKEWELL]
"You know, I wouldn't be opposed to hittin'
a ball and fallin' dead on the way down to
first base. I wouldn't be opposed to that at
all. That's a nice way to go."

GEORGE IS PLAYING CATCHER. THE NEXT BATTER HITS THE BALL HARD, TOO. GEORGE THROWS OFF HIS MASK AND TWIRLS HIS CAP HALF WAY AROUND, AS HE TRIES TO COVER HOME PLATE, LOOKING FOR ALL THE WORLD LIKE AN ANTIQUE PUFF DADDY	
	George Bakewell is from that generation of innocents for whom baseball is a game and not a bottom line. At season's end he'll turn 100.
WHILE WAITING FOR THE THROW HOME, HE YELLS	[BAKEWELL] "I've had a wonderful life."
	For Today, Bob Dotson, NBC News, with The Boys of Winter, in St. Petersburg, Florida.

HOW TO END A STORY

Find a strong visual close whenever possible. An unforgettable image, a picture that you can't top. Something you can build toward throughout the story. Something that an audience won't forget. Then, like a good poet, help the viewer understand the story's meaning. Summarize the point of the piece with a precise closing line.

A fellow by the name of Ed Panzer reminded me of that the other day. Ed and his four brothers rattled across America in the fall of 1922. They were part of a remarkable odyssey—one hundred thousand children—plucked from the slums of New York City and sent west to a new life. Most—like the Panzers—were the sons and daughters of immigrants, found starving and alone, sleeping on the streets.

The Children's Aid Society swept them up and shipped them to towns all across the country.

At each stop their arrival was advertised. The kids trooped off the train. Lined up. Couples simply picked the one they wanted. Orphans were often separated from their brothers and sisters. If an adopted child acted up, he was put on the next train west.

In Tekamah, Nebraska, four of the Panzer boys were chosen. One was not. George, the youngest, clung to Harold and refused to let them take him back to the train. So Harold stayed. But each of the five brothers went to live on a different farm. One couple wanted to adopt two of them. The brothers refused. They had made a pact to keep their last name so they would never lose track of each other. And they did not.

In the midst of the Great Depression, Ed became a doctor. Harold did too. They worked to put each other through medical school.

Brother Jack built the hospital where Harold opened his practice.

Bob became pastor of one of the largest Methodist churches in California.

And George, the baby whose hug kept the brothers together? They all started him in business. Today he is a millionaire.

When Harold Panzer turned eighty-one, he got married—with the help of his brothers. Bob performed the service. Ed was best man.

How can you summarize lives like that? As I said, Ed Panzer gave me a clue. "We've always been close," he said, pointing to his brothers. "We've always been there for each other." I turned that cliché into this closing line:

> The brothers have now, what they had
> then—each other.

Story—The Building Blocks

Words

Each section of your story should have three ideas with just enough information to help them stick in a viewer's memory. Polish these points until they shine clearly. Be hard on yourself as a writer. Say nothing in script your viewers would already know or that the visuals say more eloquently.

Pictures

Throughout the story, build your report around sequences—two or three shots of a guy buying basketball tickets; two or three shots of a husband and wife drinking coffee at a kitchen table, etc.

Silence

Stop writing occasionally and let compelling action occur without voice over. For the writer, nothing is more difficult to write than silence. For viewers, sometimes, nothing is more moving than that moment of silence.

Natural Sound

Watching news on TV is like trying to count boxcars. Too much news rattles past us, leaving little impression. How can you get people to pay attention? Use natural sound. A short blast of a horn. A cry of grief. A crowd's roar. Many people listen to TV news; they don't look at it. They're busy brushing their teeth, fixing dinner, answering the phone. We have no captive audience. No darkened theater. The only one hanging on your every word is the news director. Natural sound tells the viewer to turn toward the screen and pay attention.

Use natural sound to heighten realism, authenticity, believability; to heighten the viewer's sense of vicarious participation in the events you are showing. Some reports merely let you watch what happened. The best let you experience what went on.

Soundbites

Short soundbites prove the story you are showing. Don't use long soundbites as substitutes for more effective storytelling.

Graphics

Graphics are effective to illustrate complex ideas and story points without pictures, but don't overuse them. Find ways on location to illustrate information. Assigned a market basket story? Price of beef going up? Go to the butcher shop and ask to see some stew meat. Not steak. Stew meat, like most people can afford. Take out a five dollar bill and ask, "How much of this meat could I have bought for five dollars in 1980? Then, ask how much five dollars would buy now. The butcher takes his cleaver. Whack. He trims away the meat you can no longer afford for five dollars. That patty now looks like an hors d'oeuvre. No spinning numbers or graphics. Gloriously low-tech, yet instantly clear. That's inflation!

All television news stories have basic building blocks:

- Pictures
- Natural sound
- Logical editing, both visually and verbally
- Short soundbites
- Graphics
- Reporter on-camera standups

Sometimes pictures take precedence, sometimes soundbites or graphics. Depends on the story, but the building blocks from which you choose remain the same.

THE "SO WHAT?" TEST

A trailer home burned down. Such a story fails to meet the "So what?" test. The trailer home burned down because the walls were filled with flammable insulation describes the larger issue and meets the "So what?" test. Stories can take on a mind-numbing sameness unless they are put into context. A hurricane hits. "Damage will be in the billions." Tornadoes. "Damage could top one billion." Damage always seems to top one billion. You can almost see the audience's eyes glazing over.

Look for the telling detail that makes each story unique. If you're writing, you're watching. The material is all around you. Halifax County, North Carolina, once had a terrible flood. Government press releases said, "Damage in the billions." What does that mean? Well, it means more than those cold numbers would imply. Halifax County had fifty-five thousand people at the time. If the cost of that flood were spread evenly, every man, woman and child would lose twenty-thousand dollars. Now, *that's* a figure to which a viewer can relate. It hits the wallet. That's the price of a college tuition or a new car. Twenty-thousand dollars for every man, woman and child in Halifax County. You have added something to your story that goes way beyond a government agency handout.

Section
Three

In this age of endless live shots, we rely too much on news-release storytelling. We have to fill 24 hours. That leads to formula reporting. Live open. Voice over. Interview with the mayor. Live tag. "Back to you, Biff. I'm Bob Dotson and you're not."

Formula reporting kills communication. It either puts viewers to sleep or sends them clicking to someone else's news. People want something from your writing—understanding and insight. Look for ways to help your viewers feel something about the story and its subjects. If feeling is present, the story will be memorable. It will stick in the viewers' minds. Assigned a follow-up story? Look for file footage never before aired; unusual eyewitnesses; a different approach:

Script #7: "San Francisco Earthquake Follow"

```
"SAN FRANCISCO EARTHQUAKE
FOLLOW"/NIGHTLY NEWS
SAN FRANCISCO, CALIFORNIA
TOTAL RUNNING TIME 3:26
CORRESPONDENT:    BOB DOTSON
PRODUCER:         DAVE RIGGS
```

[LEAD MATERIAL] For most of us disasters become just clippings in the memory, something to mark the calendar of lives. But for those who lived through the Bay area earthquake in 1989, the tremors still rumble ... deep within the mind ... as Bob Dotson found out when he checked back with some of the folks he met during the tragic hours after that quake.

=-=-=-=-=-=-=-=-script-=-=-=-=-=-=-=

DEBBIE AND TOM KELLY'S VAN CROSSING BRIDGE	
DEBBIE KELLY BEGINS TALKING VOICE OVER	"My stomach goes down to my toes. I break out in a cold sweat sometimes."
	Debbie Kelly STILL cannot cross a bridge without flinching.
QUICK CUTS FROM THE KELLYS' HOME VIDEO TAKEN ON THE BAY BRIDGE DURING THE EARTHQUAKE	"Oh, Gosh."
	She and her husband were on vacation— high over San Francisco Bay—just as the earthquake struck.
DISSOLVE TO BAY BRIDGE	
EARTHQUAKE BEGINS	
BROKEN BRIDGE AERIAL	A section of the Bay Bridge dropped like a deadly trapdoor.
HOME VIDEO CAMERA MOVING TO BACK OF VAN	The Kellys turned their van to warn others.

DEBBIE KELLY VOICE OVER	"My husband tried to flash the lights and honk the horn and wave his hands and whatever else."
CAR PLUNGES INTO HOLE. DEBBIE REACTS	"GOSH! Thomas, we need to get down there and help."
DISSOLVE TO ANNA HALANGAHU'S PIX	They could not. Anna Halangahu died.
DISSOLVE TO KELLY'S VAN PASSING OKLAHOMA OIL WELL	
STANDUP	The Kellys drove home to Oklahoma, then turned around and came back. They couldn't sleep. Needed to reassure themselves that the city would recover.
SUPER: BOB DOTSON SAN FRANCISCO (_:__–_:__)	
CABLE CARS AND RECONSTRUCTED NEIGHBORHOODS	Physically, it has.
REBUILDING MARINA DISTRICT	Only in the Marina District are the wounds still on the surface.
FIRE AND FALLING BUILDINGS	The neighborhood is built on a landfill that shook like jelly.
DISSOLVE TO TWISTED HOUSE. AIDEEN MURPHY VOICE OVER AS SHE ENTERS	"I very much wanted to see what happened inside the building. I would have died of curiosity not knowing."
MURPHY DOWN ALLEY AND UP STAIRS	Everything Aideen Murphy owned was 4 flights up these rickety stairs.

POLICE RIBBONS OUTSIDE APARTMENT BUILDING	Police lines warned people not to risk their lives.
DISSOLVE TO PIX OF AIDEEN WHEN SHE WAS YOUNG	But Aideen had lived through a thousand air raids in World War Two London.
AIDEEN ASKS FOR HELP WHILE MOVING BOOKCASE	"Can I get some help here?"
AIDEEN VOICE OVER SEARCH	
BOX OF PIX	Aideen found her children's photographs and something she had bought just the week before...
OPENS CHINA CABINET	"That's incredible!"
DISSOLVE TO TEA PARTY TODAY	2 thousand dollars worth of Wedgwood china.
DOTSON OBSERVES	"It's not leaking."
AIDEEN ANSWERS	"Nope."
	The CHINA is still here today...
KEN NELSON WALKING ALONG WHAT WAS I-880	But nothing remains of 26-thousand tons of freeway. Ken Nelson watched it crumble, trapping 42 people in a concrete coffin.
INTERCUT WITH FLASHBACK SHOTS	
NELSON VOICE OVER	"I still smell the smoke. I still see the blood. I still see the crushed cars. I see the kids dead."
	And 40 who lived ... Because Nelson led an army of his neighbors to their rescue.

CONNIE BISHOP LAST YEAR	One of those he saved was a nurse, Connie Bishop.
CONNIE AND KEN HUG	"Oh, it's good to see you!"
AERIAL OF COLLAPSED FREEWAY	She was passing through West Oakland when more than a mile of double-deck highway pancaked under her.
CONNIE BISHOP ON CAMERA	"I didn't have any choice. He CHOSE to do what he did. And it is the people sometimes who are the rescuers who have the most problems after an event like this. Not those of us who were on there."
CRIPPLED FREEWAY COMES CRASHING DOWN REVEALING CARS CRUSHED LIKE PAPER CUPS	It is harder to be brave the day after. After reason returns and reveals the odds.
NELSON IN APARTMENT	Nelson got sick and lost his job.
NELSON VOICE OVER	"I still don't sleep. I lay down and I hear the screams. I hear the cries. And NOBODY would listen! I'd say, 'Hey! I need some help.'"
PUTTING PIECES OF CITY BACK TOGETHER. A SERIES OF DISSOLVES. THEN AND NOW	It is easier to put the pieces of a city back together than it is the lives of those who live there.
RESCUING PEOPLE	But—in 1989—the people of the Bay area set a new standard of caring.

KEN AND CONNIE SIT ON BAYSIDE
PARK BENCH. SHE'S COMFORTING
HIM.   And it continues.

                                        Bob Dotson, NBC News, Oakland.

ASK YOURSELF, "WHAT DOES THIS STORY MEAN?"

Occasionally step back and ask, "What does this story mean?" Is there more than meets the eye? For instance, why do children on a small island off the coast of South Carolina write wonderful poetry?

"Life changes slowly. There are no paved roads, no street lights, no bridge to the outside. Daufuskie Island is so remote, the mind can be your best friend."

These 28 words tell a great deal. You can, too, when you ask, "What am I seeing here?"

STORIES WITH NO PICTURES

What if you don't have any pictures? What then? After the O.J. Simpson trial, judges all over the country barred cameras from their courtrooms. I had to cover a big trial in South Carolina. To produce fifty-nine stories in thirty-three days with nothing but soundbites, narration and paint. Fortunately, I worked with a wonderful courtroom artist—Betty Wells:

Script #8: "Susan Smith Trial"

This story was assigned on a Friday night after the trial ended. The executive producer of the *NBC Nightly News* called me and said, "Hey, Bob, can you write me a four-minute wrap-up? I know you're tired, but it's not due until Monday." A couple of minutes later, the *Today* show's executive producer rang. "Hey, Bob. Can you put together a final piece to put a cap on this story? Take all the time you need. You can run four, five minutes. It's not due until Monday." He hung up. The phone rang again. "Hi, Bob." It was the executive producer of *Weekend Nightly News*. I'll need a long take-out on the trial for Sunday's show. You busy?"

There I sat. Exhausted. Facing three long pieces in the next sixty hours. And all we had were courtroom sketches and file tape. No new interviews and not likely to get them. The town wanted us out of there. Even CNN was gone. Yet, we needed to make thirteen minutes of news and each piece had to be different. I sat down with field producers and crews, "Okay, gang. Let's shoot and edit each of these epics with a different style. Each story will be similar, but visually we can make them look different." That's important when you have to spin the same facts into several different programs. No executive producer wants to think he got the C-plus effort.

"SUSAN SMITH TRIAL: TOWN DENIAL" /
NIGHTLY NEWS
UNION, SOUTH CAROLINA
TOTAL RUNNING TIME 4:40
CORRESPONDENT: BOB DOTSON
PRODUCER: SYLVIE OBER-
                   LANDER

[TOM BROKAW INTRO]
Time now for NBC News In-Depth. Tonight: after the Susan Smith trial ... the little town of Union, South Carolina trying to put itself back together. A community whose darkest secrets of murder, incest and illicit affairs at the top of the establishment were suddenly exposed to the world. Will Union ever be the same? NBC's Bob Dotson has our in-depth report.

=-=-=-=-=-=-=-=-script-=-=-=-=-=-=-=

TV CREWS PACKING UP OUTSIDE
UNION, SOUTH CAROLINA,
COURTHOUSE

After Big News, the world moves on—to
other places, other problems.

WOMAN ON STREET

"I'M GLAD IT'S OVER WITH. MAYBE WE
CAN BE LEFT ALONE AND GO BACK
TO OUR WAY OF LIVING."

But Union may not be able to do that. For
a month its secrets were broadcast in
unflinching, graphic detail. The town's
problems laid bare. And worst of all ... in
this close-knit village where most
EVERYONE is related ... NO ONE kept
Susan Smith from being sexually abused
as a child.

RADIO TALK SHOW HOST
SOT HENDERSON

SOT HENDERSON: THERE WERE NO
RUMORS. THERE WERE NO RUMORS.

WBCU RADIO SEQ.

SOT HENDERSON: "OOOOWEEE."

SOT HENDERSON V/O SOT: SEVEN
MINUTES PAST EIGHT O'CLOCK. CALL
IN IF YOU WANT TO."

Not a single caller to Union's "Coffee
Sipper" show said they knew her
stepfather, Bev Russell, had molested her
when she was 15.

SOT HENDERSON

"THAT WAS A SHOCK, THE
COURTSHIP SHE HAD, THAT SHE SAID
SHE HAD. THAT WAS A SHOCK."

EXT. COURT HOUSE MOODY MOVES WARD SKETCH BECOMES VIDEO	But no one in Union is talking about pressing charges. Social worker Jenny Ward testified she tried. But former Sheriff William Jolly told her the matter was closed. The case was sealed. Its file disappeared.
SOT DEBORAH GREENE	SOT GREENE: "IT WAS TAKEN CARE OF AND JENNY WAS STOPPED IN HER TRACKS. IT'S NOTHING THAT JENNY WARD DID. SHE DID EVERYTHING AND EVEN WENT BEYOND THAT."
	Susan hinted to her teacher, Deborah Greene, there were problems at 13.
SOT GREENE	SOT GREENE: "OUR HANDS WERE TIED, YOU KNOW, TIED BY THE LAW."
ART DIZ TO VIDEO	Even now Department of Social Services rules won't allow Jenny Ward to talk about Susan's case.
SOT JENNY WARD	SOT WARD: "NONE OF US IN THIS COMMUNITY WILL BENEFIT BY POINTING FINGERS AT ONE ANOTHER."
	People here prefer to keep problems to a whisper.
DOTSON STANDUP HIT TIME 1:41	[DOTSON STANDUP COPY] "THE SUSAN SMITH MURDER TRIAL TORE AT THE SOUL OF THIS TOWN. HER LIFE SENTENCE DID LITTLE TO RELIEVE THE PAIN. PEOPLE HERE STILL CANNOT BELIEVE SOMEONE SO LIKE—THEM—COULD DO SUCH AN EVIL THING."

SOT: BELLS CHIME

SOT REV. CURRIE DELIVERING A SERMON	SOT REV. CURRIE:
FIRST PRESBYTERIAN CHURCH	"MURDER IS SIN, ADULTERY IS A SIN, SEXUAL ABUSE IS A SIN, BETRAYAL IS A SIN."
CHURCH STEEPLE SEQ.	In a town of 10 thousand with 130 churches, people tend to be forgiving. That's how Union got its name. Baptists, Methodists and Presbyterians put aside their differences to worship in a single church.
TOWN OLD IMAGERY SEQ FLAGS W/ROCKERS	During the Civil War they stood together again ... and kept their homes from Sherman's torch. SOT PARISH: "AMEN"
REFLEX IN GLASS	Now they must look each other in the eye, to save themselves.
SOT SHERIFF WELLS	SOT WELLS: "TWO COUNTS OF MURDER." (CROWD GASPS) Howard Wells, the Sheriff who led the search for Smith's little boys, has words to lead them again.
SOT WELLS	SOT WELLS: "IF WE SEE SIGNS IN THE FUTURE OF SOMETHING THAT'S BEEN REPRESENTED HERE, MAYBE WE WILL LOOK AT IT DIFFERENTLY. MAYBE WE WILL REACT DIFFERENTLY AND TRY TO GIVE PEOPLE THE HELP THAT THEY NEED."

	SOT:BURGERS SIZZLE
	But some STILL deny there was a problem.
COOK AT BARBQUE RESTAURANT	SOT GENE: "I'M GONNA LOOK AT HER JUST LIKE I HAVE ALWAYS, A NICE SWEET TEENAGE, NICE POLITE GIRL."
CUSTOMER	SOT ODELL: "I THINK PEOPLE BLAME CIRCUMSTANCES."
INNOCENT TOWN	Even after all Susan did, already her hometown remembers her ... as she was before.
SOT FREEH	SOT FREEH: "I DON'T THINK AS A WHOLE, YOU'D FIND THAT GOING ON IN THIS TOWN."
SOT DR. HAROLD MORGAN	SOT DR.MORGAN: "LURKING INSIDE ALL OF US IS THE POTENTIAL FOR SOMETHING LIKE THIS."
	Psychiatrist, Dr. Harold Morgan:
SOT MORGAN	SOT DR. MORGAN: "IT'S ALMOST LIKE A DOMINO EFFECT , WHEN ONE FAMILY IS SO DYSFUNCTIONAL THEN THAT SPILLS OVER INTO ANOTHER FAMILY."
W/S RAINDROPS BEGIN OVER LAKE	
T/S RAINDROPS ON WATER	The pain is there ... just below the surface.

SOT CURTIS JACKSON, DIVER WHO FOUND SMITH'S CHILDREN	SOT JACKSON: "WHEN MAMA DOES IT TO YOU, THERE AIN'T NOBODY ELSE TO TURN TO. THOSE KIDS WERE TRULY ALONE"

SUBMERGED CAR SEQ
  W/S CAR ROLLS DOWN HILL
  INT CAR—SPLASH IN H20
  UNDERWATER SHOTS
	Curtis Jackson did not watch when prosecutors showed how the children drowned.

	SOT JACKSON: "SICKENING FEELING..."
	He already knew. Jackson was the diver who found a tiny hand pressed against glass.
SOT JACKSON	SOT JACKSON: "I HIT IT AND I KNEW THEY WERE IN THERE ... I JUST COULDN'T GET OVER HOW PEACEFUL THEY LOOKED, JUST LIKE THEY WAS ... I TRY TO FORGET, HOPEFULLY IT WILL GO AWAY."
	SOT: BIRDS
INNOCENT TOWN SHOTS	The babies are dead. Susan is in prison. David left town. And Bev Russell, the stepfather who had sex with Susan for 8 years? He's still here. Quietly working his way back into Republican politics.
SOT TRANSMISSION	SOT: CAR
	Union desperately wants to forgive. It is already trying to forget.

Bob Dotson, NBC News, Union, South
Carolina.

[TOM BROKAW TAG]
And in every small town in America
tonight, residents—comfortable in the
sanctuary of their familiar surroundings—
are wondering, "what's going on here we
don't know about?"

INVESTIGATIVE STORYTELLING

Writing longer series pieces requires an entirely different format from day-to-day news. You must build each segment with a cliffhanger ending, enticing viewers to stay tuned:

Script #9: "Top Cop"

"TOP COP" / NIGHTLY NEWS
CHARLESTON, SOUTH CAROLINA
TOTAL RUNNING TIME 3:34
CORRESPONDENT: BOB DOTSON
PRODUCER: DAVE RIGGS

FLYING SQUAD TRAINING   These cops are in training for a deadly
                                     competition.

                                     GRUNTS

                                     They are called the Flying Squad.

ROUSTING DRUG DEALERS	"HEY, COME BACK HERE!"
	It's their job to chase street kids who sell drugs.
KIDS SCURRYING AWAY	
POLICEMAN TAKING PICTURES	Joe Gabe carries an unusual weapon.
	CLICK
KIDS RUN FROM STREET CORNER	He shoots snapshots ... to scare away the dope dealers' customers.
POLICEMAN HOLDS A KID'S SNAPSHOT	"THIS PICTURE IS GOING IN MY FILE."
FRISKING SUSPECTS	Why not just arrest them?
CHIEF VOICE OVER	"IT DOESN'T DO ANY GOOD, ARRESTING THEM. 4 HOURS LATER. BACK ON THE STREET."
DOTSON AND CHIEF WALKING	Charleston police chief Reuben Greenberg says this is cheaper and just as effective as a squad of detectives gathering evidence.
FLYING SQUAD ROUNDS UP KIDS	
CHARLESTON POLICE CHIEF, REUBEN GREENBERG, ON CAMERA	"YOU DESTROY THAT CORNER AS A PLACE WHERE DRUGS CAN BE SOLD, IT WON'T MATTER IF HE'S OUT OF JAIL OR NOT. HE CAN'T MAKE A LIVING THERE."
PATROLMAN TIPTOES PAST BARKING DOG	"IS HE FRIENDLY?"
	When the pushers move indoors, Willie Robinson drops by.

PEERS OVER FENCE	"WHY YOU MOVING OUT, MAN? YOU DON'T LIKE THE AREA?"
PATROLMAN WILLIE ROBINSON ON CAMERA	"THEY DON'T LIKE THAT AT ALL, BUT THEN, THEY CAN'T DO ANYTHING ABOUT IT. WE'RE JUST BEING FRIENDLY. AS COPS SUPPOSED TO BE. (GRIN) REAL FRIENDLY."
SQUAD CAR: DAY-TO-NIGHT TRANSITION	The Flying Squad can't catch everyone, so they concentrate on keeping the seller and customers apart.
TRAFFIC CHECK	"STOP AT THE STOP SIGN, PLEASE."
	At night they set up road blocks outside known drug-buying areas. If drivers don't know who they are going to see, they are invited to leave.
COP TALKING TO DRIVER	"WE'RE GOING TO TURN YOU AROUND RIGHT HERE. YOU DON'T HAVE ANY BUSINESS IN BAYSIDE MANOR."
COPS WALKING IN DARK ALLEY	If they do know, the cops go with them to see who's home.
POLICE CRUISER RACES UP. SUSPECT IS SPREAD-EAGLED AGAINST WALL. COP COMMANDS HIM TO OPEN HIS HAND AND SHOW WHAT HE IS TIGHTLY CLUTCHING. A POLICE DOG SNIFFS FOR DRUGS. A SMALL PLASTIC BAG, SUSPECTED OF CONTAINING DOPE, POPS OUT	"OPEN UP! OPEN UP!" The Charleston Police are fighting this drug war with every law on the books. "TELL ME, WHAT IS THAT?" "HUH?" "YOU TELL ME, WHAT IS THAT! TURN AROUND."

WRITING A TICKET	Suspected dealers have even been cited for littering.
ARRESTS	If they fail to show up in court, the cops get a warrant, then arrest them on Friday nights.
CHIEF REUBEN GREENBERG ON CAMERA	"BECAUSE THERE'S NO BOND. HE CAN BE A MILLIONAIRE. CAN'T GET OUT. HE'S GOT TO WAIT UNTIL MONDAY MORNING. SO YOU JUST REACHED HIM. BOOM. TOOK A WHOLE WEEKEND AWAY FROM HIM WITH WHAT TURNED OUT TO BE THE LITTERING VIOLATION HE DIDN'T PAY."
SUSPECT BEING FRISKED COMPLAINS	"YES, THIS IS THE UNITED STATES HERE. THIS IS THE DRUG ATTACK FORCE, D.E.A."
PATROLMAN JOE GABE	"DON'T YOU LOVE IT?"
SUSPECT	"CHARLESTON, SOUTH CAROLINA."
COP HOLDS SUSPECT	No police brutality lawsuits have been filed since Greenberg took over.
WILLIE ROBINSON CARRYING BABY	The cops have been trained not to treat everyone like a suspect.
SQUAD CARS IN HOT PURSUIT. CHIEF GREENBERG IS DRIVING ONE OF THEM. AMBULANCE RACES PAST	If they break something in hot pursuit, they will come back and fix it. For free.
CHIEF TALKING TO SUSPECT'S NEIGHBORS	The Chief doesn't run neighbors away from a crime scene. Instead he asks their help.

GREENBERG: "JUST TELL HIM TO COME ON OVER TO THE STATION."

STANDUP: DOTSON IN PROJECTS

SUPER: BOB DOTSON
     CHARLESTON, S.C.
     (_:__-_:__)

How well is it working? Charleston's crime rate is the lowest it's been in 25 years. There are about half as many murders, robberies and burglaries. By disrupting these daily drug deals, even public housing projects seem safer. Only one person has been shot and killed in 5 years.

COP CAR DOWN STREET. YOUNG COUPLE OUT WALKING BABY WATCH IT GO BY

In some inner cities police are seen as an army of occupation. In Charleston, they are liberators.

SUPER: WILHELMINA JONES
     (_:__-_:__)

"WE'RE NOT GOING TO LET THE HOODLUMS RUN US OUT. WE'RE GOING TO RUN THEM OUT. THAT'S THE WAY WE FEEL ABOUT IT."

COP CAR ROLLS TO STOP AT STREET CORNER. PEOPLE SCATTER. PAY PHONE IS RINGING. PATROLMAN JOE GABE ANSWERS. TURNS CALLS OUT NAME. EVERYONE IS GONE. HE INSISTENTLY QUESTIONS THE CALLER

A decade ago Charleston had drug dealers on 35 corners. Today someone else may be taking those calls.

"FLIP FLAP? IS FLIP FLAP HERE?"

The uncertainty is terrible for business.

"DO YOU NEED ANYTHING?"

Bob Dotson, NBC News, Charleston, South Carolina.

"DO YOU NEED ANYTHING ELSE?"

We'll Be Right Back...

Flip Flap called so often, we had time to get a dozen different angles of Officer Gabe asking the question, "Do you need anything?" What makes that funny is the cop waiting for Flip Flap to answer, so I timed that pause in the edit room. Found it was five seconds. When I scripted my final line of narration, I wrote it to fit into the pause. I wanted to make sure that my words would slip into the pause between Officer Gabe's question and Flip Flap's answer. That was essential to keep the funny timing of the scene.

Don't shorten a moment like that. If you change its timing, it won't be funny. Such moments are crucial in setting up the cliffhanger ending. Get the viewer to laugh at the end of a serious story, and they'll tune in for part two.

EDITING STORIES

Some people think that if you rewrite, it means you are an amateur. But, professionals constantly tweak what they have written. The edit console is your best rewrite machine. It is not just where you take out the bad parts. It is where you begin the deliberate process of guiding viewer thoughts and associations. All the building blocks you've gathered—sound, picture, information—are of equal value in the edit room. Like a beautiful building, each block has its place. But, don't overproduce your piece. Create lovely images with words when you can, but realize the kind of painting that is possible, given the time. Most days you won't have time for a richly textured piece. Whittle down your shooting and your scripting. This economy leaves more time to work on a *few* things—pretty pictures, good natural sound, memorable soundbites, clever editing, economical writing and reporting.

REPORTING VS. STORYTELLING

Remember: *reporting* and *storytelling* are two sides of the same coin. You can't be effective in television unless you master both. Unfortunately, some in our business see them at odds with each other. Reporting is what you do to get a great story, but stories are remembered only if you tell them well.

CAR WARS

I got my first big time job back when the earth was cooling. Stepped into the NBC News bureau in Cleveland, Ohio, during the snowiest winter in American history ... 1975. The first person I met was a whiskery little soundman named Frank Greene. We were standing on a chilly sidewalk waiting for a crew car to take us to an assignment. Frank somehow managed to maintain a two-inch ash on the cigarette dangling from the corner of his mouth, as he greeted me with one eye squinting through smoke that drifted up his face. "I just want youse ta know one 'ting," he said, his voice a low rasp. "I've been here thirty years and I'll *be* here when you're gone!" Frank was nearing retirement. He must have had underwear older than I was.

Coming up through small stations, I had seldom worked with anyone over thirty. Didn't know what to say. Frank wasn't expecting an answer. He was telling me what to expect. "When we go out on stories, I sits in the right front seat." A stiff breeze finally knocked the ash off Frank's cigarette. "I always sits next to the heater." He paused to puff. "The cameraman drives, unless he doesn't want to. Then, the electrician drives. Otherwise, the electrician—who we call 40-watt, cuz he's usually a dim bulb—he sits in the back seat on the hump." Another puff. Frank smoked Camels. Once he lit a cigarette, it stayed in the corner of his mouth until he took it out to light another. Frank glanced at the crew car garage. No sign yet of our ride. He continued, "The producer always sits in the back left seat, behind the driver, so he can flick 'im on the ear and tell 'im to turn right or left."

A small smile. "You? Reporters sit in the right rear seat." He wiggled his index finger. "Don't crowd 40-watt." The crew car pulled to the curb. Frank popped into the front seat next to the heater. "Welcome to Cleveland," he said, pointing to my place in back.

This was the first time that I had ever worked with a guy who cared more about heat than TV. At noon I learned he cared about food, too. "Hey, Dotson," he rasped. "Youse got ten more minutes!"

"Ten minutes until what, Frank?"

"Ten minutes, den I'm pulling my audio plug and sittin' in da car until we go to lunch."

We were filming children on a playground. True to his word, ten minutes later, Frank yanked his audio line from the back of the camera and left. I looked at cameraman Cliff Adkins. Cliff shrugged.

"Well," said Cliff. "At least Frank waited until we got a minute's worth of audio in the can. No one can fault him for not doing his job."

I looked around glumly. "Yeah, but what are we going to do?" Was this the end of my big-time career?

"Do you want to drive Frank nuts?" asked Cliff.

I grinned. "Sure."

"He's going to expect one of two things," said Cliff. "Either we yell at him when we go back to the car or we give him the silent treatment."

I nodded. Made sense.

"If you really want to drive him crazy," said Cliff, "let's act like nothing ever happened."

"How will that drive him crazy?"

"You see, he wants to pick a fight so he can file a union grievance," Cliff said. That'll take him out of the cold for days while the grievance sorts itself out. Meanwhile, he'll be warm and get lunch on time."

"Why doesn't he just talk to the managers who assign the story? It's not our fault he's working through lunch."

"He's afraid," said Cliff. "It's easier and safer to take out his frustration on us."

"Great," I sighed.

"Well, let's do it," said Cliff. "Let's pretend as if nothing ever happened, but you have to promise me one thing."

"What's that."

"You've got to talk to the assignment editor and remind him that Frank needs his lunch on time. Food and heat are important when you're over sixty." Cliff grinned, but he meant it.

We finished our shooting, then walked back to the crew car. Frank was hunkered down in the front seat, next to the heater. Engine running.

"Hi, Frank!" I said. "Hey, where do you want to go eat?"

Two weeks later, we worked together again. We met on that same chilly corner. Frank was pacing back and forth.

"Hi, Frank..."

"All right!" Frank growled. "What's goin' on!"

"Going on? What, Frank?"

"How come youse never yelled at me?"

"Yell at you, Frank? Why?"

"You know why!"

"Well," I said. "I thought you made a good point about missing lunch, so I talked to the assignment editor when I got back to make sure you didn't miss any more."

"You did?"

"Yeah."

"Oh."

Frank Greene was not our best soundman. He was known for letting the needle ride in the red. Didn't pay much attention to over-modulation. But, from that day forward he got better when he worked with me. I always made sure to highlight Frank's audio in my stories. If he climbed down a hill to get sound of a rushing river, I would pause in my narration to let the sound play. Gradually, grudgingly, we became friends.

My wife, Linda, was five months pregnant at the time. The day she flew from Oklahoma to join me in our new home, I met her at the airport with Frank and the crew. We were on our way to Cincinnati, assigned to do a *Today* show story. Would she care to fly along in the Lear jet?

"What's another plane ride?" said Linda.

Off we went.

When we arrived in Cincinnati, 40-watt pulled the rental car alongside the plane. Frank hopped out and opened the car door. The front passenger door.

"Mrs. Dotson," he motioned. "Would youse like to sit next to da heater?"

The next morning, over coffee, Cliff Adkins shook his head.

"I've worked for thirteen years with Frank Greene and I've never seen Frank give up the heater. Not even for a pregnant *nun*!"

"Cliff," I asked? "Why is it we are paid because we communicate clearly with thousands of people every day, but we can't seem to talk to the guy sitting next to us in the crew car? It's so important that each of us work well together because the result is a group effort. Seems to me the water walkers who sign paychecks don't know good audio from bad or great camerawork from home video. All they say is, 'That story wasn't wonderful.'"

"We seldom work well together," said Cliff, "because we blame everyone else while overlooking our own failures. I say, 'My story would have been an award winner, but you wrote wall-to-wall narration.' You say, 'Hey, Cliff, your shots are shaky and the audio is unusable.' Remember, Bob, the only person you can change is yourself. You want to get better. Make yourself better by helping others to be better, too. People who help you survive in this business are not always the most pleasant. Don't waste your life waiting to work with the "best" or cursing your fate when faced with a "Frank Greene." Frank became a good friend and we made each other better than we thought we could be.

Think of this business as a rough-and-tumble football game. View life like a broken field runner. Change when you see an opening. Then, try to make yourself one of a kind. You might not get every assignment you want, but someday, someone will say ...

"We need a Bob Dotson story..."

Some day they will think of you ... first.

Reporter's Checklist

I hope you've found some ideas in this book that make it worth its price. In closing, I pass along my "Reporter's Checklist," questions I ask myself during every assignment:

- ❏ How can I make this a compelling story with universal values that appeal to a wide audience?

- ❏ Where can I find a strong opening, preferably a visual lead, that instantly telegraphs the story to come?

- ❏ Is my writing strong, tight, free of information that people would already know?

- ❏ Does the story build to a close?

- ❏ Are there elements of surprise within the visuals or sound to attract and hold viewers?

❑ Is the subject matter interesting, concrete, important—not just another fluff piece?

❑ Does my piece meet and answer the "So what?" test? Does it contain historical perspective that defines the story's larger context? Does it address a larger issue?

❑ Is my story told through people engaged in compelling action that is visual or picturesque? Does the report let people tell their own story whenever possible?

❑ Did I let the camera "talk" for itself whenever possible?

❑ Is my camerawork steady? Do I have a creative treatment of content and composition; interesting angles; minimal use of pans and zooms? How well does my camerawork meet professional and creative standards?

❑ Are my on-camera appearances, if any, used appropriately and not used to substitute for more compelling elements of the story?

❑ Do my standup appearances deliver information that helps drive the story forward?

❑ Are my voice-over narrations delivered with authority, spontaneity, feeling? Are they tight, active voice, understandable, readable, listenable?

❑ Does the soundtrack carry meaning that can help viewers create secondary visual images (subtext)?

❑ Is my audio quality crisp and clean? Am I using wild sound and background sound and soundbites to break up long narration?

❑ Is the music, if any, appropriate to mood and content?

❐ Is my lighting natural? Can I use available light? Does it highlight what I want the viewer to notice?

❐ Does my editing give the story pace? Am I building the story in a logical sequence? Am I matching its action? Does it cut smoothly from wide shot to close-up? Do my soundtracks overlap smoothly? No dead air? Do I have a picture or graphic to cover everything I need to say?

A FINAL THOUGHT

Sometimes the answer to those questions will be "No," or "Not much." We all have bad hands dealt us every day, because shorter deadlines and increasing story counts have us working faster and longer.

Just remember—success in this business does not depend on being dealt a good hand. It's playing a bad hand well, over and over again.

Index